Young People and Chronic Illness

True Stories, Help, and Hope

KELLY HUEGEL

Foreword by Robert H. Phillips, Ph.D.

free spirit
PUBLISHING®
Works
for kids™

Library of Congress Cataloging-in-Publication Data

Huegel, Kelly.
      Young people and chronic illness : true stories, help, and hope / by Kelly Huegel
            p.   cm.
      Includes index.
      Summary: Presents true accounts of young people living with a chronic illness including how they have learned to cope and remain hopeful; also includes strategies for living with a chronic medical problem.
      ISBN 1-57542-041-4 (pbk.)
      1. Chronic diseases in children—Juvenile literature. 2. Adjustment (Psychology) in children—Juvenile literature. [1. Diseases—Case studies. 2. Sick—Psychology. 3. Self-acceptance.] I. Verdick, Elizabeth. II. Title.
      RJ388.H84   1998
      618.92'0001'9—dc21

                                                                                      98-10439
                                                                                      CIP
                                                                                      AC

Edited by Gretchen Bratvold and Elizabeth Verdick
Cover and book design by Cindy Olson
Index prepared by Eileen Quam and Theresa Wolner

This book contains many recommendations for Web sites. Because Web sites change often and without notice, we can't promise every address listed will still be accurate when you read it. When in doubt, use a search engine.

10 9 8 7 6 5 4 3 2

Printed in the United States of America

Free Spirit Publishing Inc.
400 First Avenue North, Suite 616
Minneapolis, MN 55401-1724
(612) 338-2068
help4kids@freespirit.com
www.freespirit.com

Acknowledgments

I would like to acknowledge the help of some very special people who supported me during the months I spent writing this book.

I can think of no words to adequately express my appreciation for my family. My thanks to my parents, Jane and Dave, for their boundless love, assurance, and willingness to put up with my periodic disappearances throughout the writing of this book. Thanks also to Monica for her quiet, but ever-present, support.

Amy Ziegenfuss acted as my research assistant, writing coach, chef, gopher, motivator, best friend, and woman with whom I share a brain (thanks for letting me have it on the weekends). You were a source of strength and encouragement.

Special thanks to Laura Noss—an extremely talented person and great friend who was always generous with her time and creative gifts. My appreciation extends, as well, to my wonderful circle of friends, all of whom were there at one time or another to lend their support.

Thanks to Nancy Hicks, Leslie Whitlinger, and the Hill & Knowlton health-care specialty group—an excellent and hard-working team who always found a few more minutes in their day to help me. Thank you to my colleagues in the editorial and production departments of Taylor & Francis. Special thanks to Alison Mudditt for her good council and for traveling a long way just to be my boss. Thank you also to Elizabeth Verdick, Gretchen Bratvold, and all the helpful people at Free Spirit Publishing.

I would also like to thank the professionals who donated their time and expertise. Dr. Wanda Ruffin at Hood College, Dr. Robert Lipnick at Children's Hospital in Washington, D.C., Dr. Edward Tyson and Dr. Kendall Stanford at Children's Hospital of Oklahoma, Dr. Robert Blum at the University of Minnesota Hospital and Clinic—Division of General Pediatrics and

Adolescent Health, Dr. Robert H. Phillips of the Center for Coping, Dr. Laurence A. Boxer at the University of Michigan, Dr. Jonathan Miller, and Peg Mann Rinehart at the National Center for Youth with Disabilities. I'm also grateful to Mona Barmash at the Children's Health Information Network, Rachel Cohen, Susan Hurwitch, Judy Madden, Kathryn Nnoka, and Sandi Qualley.

Thank you to the national foundations and organizations whose diligent employees assisted me in getting in touch with the remarkable young people featured in this book. Special thanks to Tamara Calkins and the University of Maryland Medical Center.

Finally, thank you to the young people who shared their stories so that others may learn from their experiences.

Table of Contents

Foreword

"Do you know someone who has gone through life without ever having had any type of medical problem? I don't. Whether it's mild problems, such as headaches, colds, or aches and pains; minor injuries; or more serious chronic illnesses, medical problems, or injuries, virtually everyone has had something.*"*

I began my book, *Rising to the Challenge: Celebrities and Their Very Personal Health Stories,* with the passage above. Yes, it seems like every time you turn around, there's another story in the news (or in the tabloids) about a celebrity dealing with an illness. We almost expect it. We also expect that, as people grow older, illness will become more the norm than wellness.

But we don't necessarily expect that you—our adults of tomorrow—will have to go through medical illness at this point in your life. Childhood and adolescence are supposed to be a time of joy, learning, and eager anticipation of the future.

So what happens when a chronic illness enters the picture? Is it possible to live a happy life, even though you have a medical problem? Yes. And if you're wondering how, this book can tell you.

Some people seem to know how to deal with adversity better than others. They always seem to be smiling and happy, regardless of how serious their physical or emotional problems may be. Some people do this naturally; others need to work at it. Then there are those who seem to have trouble dealing with anything, especially a medical problem that may result in a lifestyle change.

Why are there differences? Because people are different. Which category do you fit into? It matters—but then again, it doesn't. The important message is this: You *can* deal with things. *Coping* is the answer. If you can cope with your medical problem—deal with it positively and constructively—despite the negatives of your situation or condition, you *can* lead a happy, achieving life. You don't have to fall apart if you don't want to. It may take effort. You may have to learn new skills. But it can be done.

If you're facing a medical problem (or any other type of problem), people may have told you, "Well, you'll just have to cope with it." But what if you don't know how? As a psychologist, I'm heavily involved in teaching my patients coping skills—the actual techniques that people can use to help themselves improve their lives. One of the things I do is to recommend books that can be an important part of the self-improvement process. You are reading such a book.

Young People and Chronic Illness can help you in a number of ways. You'll read about people who are living with chronic illness, and you'll realize that you're not alone. You'll see how these young people have coped with their illness and stayed positive. Just as importantly, you'll find chapters full of helpful strategies to assist people living with medical problems.

Get ready for an exciting adventure, both in reading this book and living your life. Always look forward. Rather than asking yourself, "Why me?" ask yourself, "What can I do?" And always remember my motto: No matter what problem you may face, you can *always* improve the quality of your life. My thoughts are with you. Good luck!

Robert H. Phillips, Ph.D., Founder and Director, Center for Coping Long Island, NY

Introduction

*"When one door of happiness closes, another opens;
but often we look so long at the closed door that we
do not see the one which has been opened for us."*
Helen Keller

When I was diagnosed at age twelve with a chronic illness, I felt as if a door had shut right in my face. It took me a long time to see that another door was opening for me. I hope that my book will guide you on *your* way to opening many new doors.

Doors are thresholds to new places. Sometimes it can be very difficult to open a door, walk through, and explore the new place. But you just might find—as I did, and as so many others have—that the new place offers many wonderful discoveries.

▲▼▲▼▲▼▲▼

Eleven years ago, I was rushed to the hospital because of severe pain in my stomach. Shortly after I awoke from surgery, I was told that I had Crohn's disease.* Crohn's is one of two inflammatory bowel

---

*For more on Crohn's disease, see pp. 72–83.

diseases (IBDs); the other is ulcerative colitis. Crohn's can affect any part of your digestive system and may cause painful infections in addition to a number of other health problems. And, as with all chronic illnesses, there's no cure.

As I was growing up, I had trouble dealing with my illness. I was ashamed and refused to discuss my health problems with anyone—especially my friends. So I often felt all the more isolated, as if I held a deep, dark secret. I had many questions about my illness. *How will my life change? Can I go to college? Will anyone ever hire me for a job? Am I going to die?* But the answers were in short supply.

At college (I did go), I finally met someone else my age who had Crohn's, and I realized that I needed to think about my illness—and myself—differently. For many years, I had thought I wasn't "normal" and that people wouldn't like me if they knew the truth about my illness. Here's what I came to realize: For me, having a chronic illness is normal. I no longer felt so isolated and ashamed. It took me a long time, but I gradually began to accept my illness.

Everyone in the world has some special characteristic or difference—something that sets them apart from others. For people with chronic illnesses, the difference may be more obvious. You'll meet many such people in this book, and you'll learn not only about their illnesses but also about the other aspects of their lives: their families, friends, talents, interests, struggles, and dreams. I hope that reading their stories will help you to redefine what you think of as "normal." You may discover that it's okay—in fact, it's a great thing—to be who you are.

How to Use This Book

Part 1, *People Like Me,* is made up of true stories from young people who have a variety of chronic illnesses. Their chronic illnesses are some of the most common among young people: arthritis, asthma, cancer, diabetes, epilepsy, congenital heart defects, hemophilia, IBD, and lupus. Following each story is a question and answer (Q & A) section about the illness, in case you want to learn more about its symptoms, effects, treatments, and more.

You may be wondering, "Just what *is* a chronic illness?" There's a lot of debate over the exact definition, so I consulted doctors and other experts to help me figure out the best working definition for this book. I use "chronic illness" to refer to medical illnesses that:

1. have no cure, but

2. are not necessarily terminal.

The doctors and counselors who acted as advisors for the book, my publisher, and I debated over the inclusion of one of the most common and frightening illnesses of our time: HIV (human immunodeficiency virus, which can lead to AIDS). In the end, I chose not to include HIV/AIDS because, despite recent advances in AIDS treatment, it's still a *terminal* illness. And, unlike chronic illnesses, HIV/AIDS is transmitted—usually from a parent, in the case of children with HIV/AIDS. Young people who have HIV/AIDS often have to cope not only with the illness as it affects them, but also as it affects those close to them. As a young person with a chronic illness, I didn't feel qualified to address the intense emotional and mental-health issues that accompany AIDS or any other terminal illness.

Terminal illnesses aren't included in this book, but I believe that terminal and chronic illness patients share similar concerns: dealing with doctors and hospitals, telling friends and other people, and managing an illness so that it's still possible to lead a happy, successful life. You'll see how these issues have affected the young people in this book and how they've learned to cope. Although not every story in Part 1 will apply directly to you, there's still plenty we can learn from each other, as I discovered while interviewing the young people for the book. Whether we have a chronic illness, a terminal illness, a friend or family member with a disease, or a clean bill of health, we're not that different. We can all learn from each other's experiences.

▲▼▲▼▲▼▲▼

Throughout Part 2, *Learning to Cope,* you'll find ideas and strategies that I wish I'd had when I was growing up with a chronic illness. At that time, I wished for a magic formula to turn my life "back to normal." Although I can't offer any magic formulas, I can provide ideas for learning to accept your illness and deal positively with adversity it may cause. I'm not a doctor or a counselor, but I consulted many medical experts while writing this book. They helped me with the information and advice, and I guarantee that I can understand what you're going through (because I've been through a lot, too).

You'll find advice on dealing with friends, family, school, and hospitals. You'll learn strategies for accepting and managing your illness, and building relationships with doctors. You'll discover the benefits of support groups and learn how to plan for life after high school, whether at work or at college. This book also contains many resource suggestions for further help (organizations, Web sites, and other books); you'll find them at the end of each story in Part 1 and in "Support Groups and National Organizations" in Part 2.

▲▼▲▼▲▼▲▼

Some of the young people featured in this book still have issues that they're struggling with. In fact, eleven years after my diagnosis, I still have a hard time dealing with some of the challenges my illness presents. Even as you begin to use positive coping strategies, life won't suddenly become easy. But the skills you'll learn in this book can help you deal with issues as they arise and make the most of the wonderful opportunities that lie ahead. Learning is a process, and learning to cope is something you'll continue to do for the rest of your life.

Don't ever let yourself believe that your illness has ruined your chances for success. Despite my illness, I graduated in the top 10 percent of my high school class, was the captain of the tennis team, and was voted most valuable tennis player. In college, I was twice voted president of my dormitory, was in the academic honors program, participated in many campus clubs and organizations, played intramural basketball, was captain of the tennis team, won most valuable player again, and graduated with honors. I decided not to let Crohn's "win." I wanted to succeed, and I didn't let two surgeries, three flare-ups, several exhausting procedures, and countless doctor visits drag me down. You'll find that the young people in this book have similar stories to share.

This may sound a little strange, but I think that my illness did a lot to help me achieve my goals. Having Crohn's disease taught me to make the most of the times when I wasn't sick and gave me an additional drive to succeed. I'm a bit stubborn, and when it comes to a challenge, it's hard for me to resist. I've always been driven to prove that my illness can't keep me from pursuing my dreams.

I was diagnosed with asthma during college and have developed arthritis as a result of my Crohn's.* I've had to accept these limitations, but I won't give up. Your illness will probably limit you physically. It's up to you whether you'll let it limit you emotionally as well. Remember that every day there are people just like you facing tough problems. I can't give you the strength to manage your illness, but I hope to give you the tools to find the strength that's already inside you and make the most of it.

Your life hasn't ended because of your diagnosis. A new one has just begun.

Kelly Huegel

*For more on asthma, see pp. 44–54; for more on arthritis, see pp. 84–93.

Part 1

People Like Me

Greg
(Hemophilia)

Greg Price is fourteen years old and in eighth grade. He has hemophilia B (factor IX deficiency), a blood disorder. Greg lives with his parents and older brother, Jeff, and enjoys fencing, swimming, and working with computers. After high school, Greg plans to go to college to study computer programming.

I was born with hemophilia, so I've never known what it's like not to have a chronic illness. I was diagnosed when I was two-and-a-half months old, when I got my first immunization shot and my whole leg swelled. To find out why this happened, the doctors did some blood tests and discovered that I have hemophilia. The shot had caused so much bleeding inside my leg that it swelled up. After that, whenever the doctor gave me a shot, he'd immediately put an ice pack on the spot to limit the bleeding.

When I tell people about my hemophilia, I explain that there are fourteen elements, called *factors,* in the blood, all of which are needed to help it to clot. People who have hemophilia are missing one or more of these factors or the factors don't function properly, so it's harder for the blood to clot. For example, if someone who doesn't have hemophilia gets bumped hard or pulls a muscle, a small amount of internal bleeding will usually result, but the bleeding stops pretty quickly. When I have internal bleeding, it takes longer to stop. I could actually end up losing a lot of blood if I don't get treated with the right factor mixture. Minor cuts aren't a problem—I just put on a Band-Aid like anyone else. I don't bleed harder or faster than other people, just longer. Since hemophilia is hereditary, no one has to worry about catching it from me—it's not contagious.

I don't have to get an *external* injury to start bleeding. Sometimes I have episodes known as "bleeds." A bleed is when your body starts bleeding internally. Sometimes the bleed is caused by an injury, but other times a bleed is called "spontaneous" because there's no apparent cause. Bleeds happen mainly in joints, but they can also occur in organs. I know when I'm having a bleed because that area starts to hurt. I feel heat and pressure, and the spot where I'm bleeding swells.

If the bleed is in my ankles or knees, sometimes I can't walk, and I have to use crutches or a wheelchair. Everyone who has hemophilia has different target areas—places in their body where they're more likely to have bleeds. Mine are my ankles. I can get bleeds in my ankles if I'm too active or if I twist them or bump into something. That's why I can't play any contact sports—because of the chance that I'll be hit and have a bad bleed. The scariest bleeds are those that occur in the brain. I've never had a brain bleed, but whenever I hit my head I get treated with a factor, even if I don't have any symptoms.

Greg

All of my friends know about my hemophilia because I've had it for so long. When I meet new people, I just flat out tell them about my condition. That way, if I come to school on crutches because I've had a bleed in my ankles, people aren't surprised and I don't have to worry about explaining. It's just easier for me when my friends and others know.

My friends are cool about my illness, too. I know a few people who've been called names and teased after opening up about their illness. But I've never had any problems like that.

▲▼▲▼▲▼▲▼

I used to get plasma treatments when I was little. Plasma is the liquid part of the blood that contains factor. My dad donated most of the plasma, but my aunt and a few friends gave some as well. I was injected with the plasma, which improved my blood's ability to clot. The whole process took about two-and-a-half hours each time. We had to go to the hospital emergency room for the treatments, which I received about every ten days. Since plasma needs to be frozen while it's stored, we would have to wait thirty minutes just for it to thaw.

Because I grew up going to hospitals, I'm not afraid of them. Sometimes I resented having to go to the hospital so much, but it was just part of my routine—something I knew I had to do. My mom says that when I was really little, I used to cry and scream when I had to go to the hospital. I hated being stuck with a needle, and three people would have to hold me down.

When I turned three, my mom and dad told me that when I got a shot I could yell and scream as much as I wanted, as long as I sat still. So I did. When I got a little older, I just yelled, "Ouch!" Then my dad had an idea—I should blow in his face when I got a shot. If I concentrated on that, the needle didn't hurt so much. Gradually, I began to relax as I learned what hospitals were all about (helping people). I even became friends with some of the nurses, and I missed them when it was time to leave.

In fourth grade, I got a bad kidney bleed that lasted about three months off and on. I spent many days in the emergency room getting plasma, but the bleeding wouldn't stop completely. Finally, I was put on factor concentrate, and the bleeding stopped. I had my tenth birthday in the ER. The doctors and nurses, who had become my friends, felt bad that I had to be there on my birthday. So they threw a party for me and even brought presents and balloons. It was depressing to be in the hospital on my birthday, but the celebration made me feel a lot better.

After that, the nurses started giving me regular injections of a factor concentrate instead of the plasma treatments I'd been getting. With the concentrate, I only needed injections every two or three weeks (instead of every ten days for the plasma). It was great! After about a year, the nurses taught me how to give myself the treatments at home, and I've been doing the injections on my own ever since. The factor mixture comes in a powder, which I combine with sterile water. I then inject the mixture into one of my veins. The whole process takes about half an hour. Once in a while, I get frustrated because I can't get the needle in a vein. I'll try a couple of times, but if I still can't, we call a nursing service that sends a nurse to the house to help. It's a lot less of a hassle than going to the emergency room.

I missed several days of school when I had the bad kidney bleed in fourth grade, and I used to be out of school a lot when I was getting plasma treatments. Now I usually only miss school when I have bad bleeds or if I have to go in late after giving myself factor. My teachers are really good about working out revised timelines for my school work and helping me to catch up. I've been able to keep up with my classes pretty well.

Because my teachers know about my hemophilia, they understand my situation and are willing to help. At the beginning of each school year, I attend the teachers' in-service day. I introduce myself, explain that I have hemophilia, and talk about how it affects me and my life at school. I answer questions and pass out pamphlets that the teachers can take with them so they have enough information to understand my needs. I ask the teachers to treat me as they would any other student. Because everyone's always been very understanding and supportive, I don't get nervous about speaking at the in-service.

My physical education teachers tend to ask me the most questions because that's the class where my illness really comes into play. They need to know what I can and can't do. I'm able to do most of the things the other kids can do, except play contact sports or really overexert myself. I make adjustments as needed. If we're running and my ankles start to hurt, I slow down and take it easy. If there's something I really can't do, I just sit out. My teachers trust me to be honest with them about my limits.

Some shop teachers have been concerned, too—they worry that I might cut myself. In fact, I think I'm their worst nightmare! Seriously, though, I've never had any problems in shop. I just make sure that I'm very careful.

Do you want to know what bothers me most about my condition? Not being able to play any sport that I want. I've always been very active physically, but when I was little, my mom didn't let me play a lot of contact sports with my friends because she was afraid I'd get hurt. Even now, I still can't do a lot of athletics. It's rough when all of my friends are out playing a sport that I'm not allowed to participate in. I really resent my hemophilia when that happens, but I try to remind myself that life could be a lot worse. When I put things into perspective, my life doesn't seem that bad.

When I feel resentful about my hemophilia, the way I handle it is to concentrate on the things I *can* do. There are other sports I enjoy that don't involve contact, so I spend my time playing them. One of the activities I like is fencing. I started two-and-a-half years ago. At first, my mom wasn't too excited about the idea, but I kept after her until she agreed to let me take classes. Now I go to the Virginia Academy of Fencing. We wear a lot of protective gear, so I'm really not in danger of being hurt, although I do get lots of bruises. Another sport I enjoy is swimming. I've been on a swim team since I was six.

I'm also involved in Scouting. One of my worst bleeds happened at Scout camp. I fell out of a canoe, hitting the back of my leg hard. I got a huge bruise that went from above my knee down to my ankle. I should have treated the area with factor, but I didn't. My Scout leader trusted me to know what was best for me, so he took my word for it when I told him that I'd treat the injury when I got home. By the time I got back to my house three days later, I could hardly walk. I needed factor treatments for eight days to finally stop all of the bleeding. I limped and couldn't straighten my leg for three weeks. Ignoring my injury wasn't exactly the smartest thing I've ever done. My mom drove me crazy after that because she obsessed about the incident so much! Next time I get a really bad bleed, I'll take care of myself immediately and not let the bleeding go for so long.

My hemophilia has affected my relationship with my family in some ways. When my brother and I are kidding around, he doesn't punch me as hard as he could. And my parents can be overly protective because they're afraid for me. When I'm giving myself a factor treatment, for example, my mom starts to hover. I think she's nervous and wants to make sure I do it right, even though I've been giving myself the treatments for three years. I have to tell her to leave me alone, but I don't know if she'll ever be able to stop hovering. She cares about me—I know that—but things can get tense. I've even yelled at my parents, and we've gotten into fights when I'm trying to give myself the treatment. I just wish that they could trust me to take care of myself properly.

My uncle has hemophilia like me. I've learned more about my illness from him, and he's taught me a lot about my treatment. When I was little, my uncle explained to us that it was a lot safer to have family members donate blood for my plasma treatments. That way, we wouldn't have to worry about receiving blood contaminated with viruses like HIV (human immunodeficiency virus, which can lead to AIDS) and hepatitis. I find it really helpful to be able to talk to someone who has hemophilia, too—when I talk to my uncle, he knows exactly what I mean, and he understands how I feel. Sometimes he nags me if he thinks I'm not taking good care of myself, but I guess I can understand that.

▲▼▲▼▲▼▲▼

Because I administer my own treatments, I don't have to see my doctor very often. My primary doctor is a hematologist (someone who specializes in the treatment of blood disorders). I usually only see this doctor once a year when I go to the comprehensive care clinic for an examination to make sure that everything's going well. At the exam, the hematologist examines my joints and asks how everything's going with my treatments, and a nurse draws blood and talks with me about all the bleeds I've had that year. A physical therapist evaluates my joint function to see if repeated bleeding has caused any stiffness or arthritis,* and suggests exercises to strengthen the muscles around the joints so I won't bleed as easily. While I'm at my appointment, I also see a counselor about any problems or concerns I may have. All of this takes a long time, but it's worth it because I learn more about managing my hemophilia.

During the last two years, I've had the opportunity to take part in a study conducted by a local hospital. A drug company developed a new factor product but needed to test it on actual patients. I'm one of the youngest people to participate, and I inject myself with the product like I would any other factor. I knew that the most dangerous part of the study was the chance that the new factor wouldn't work—if I were to get hurt, I could end up having a serious bleed. So far, I've been taking the trial factor for two years and haven't had any problems.

---

*For more on arthritis, see pp. 84–93.

Six months into the study, the medical company that makes the new product invited me to visit the factory in Massachusetts where the factor is made. My family and I were going on vacation anyway, so we stopped in Massachusetts and toured the factory. I actually got to see the room where the factor is mixed. It was cool to see the whole process, and I was glad I'd been invited. Participating in the study has made me feel like I've made a contribution to medicine—now other hemophiliacs will have access to a new method of treatment.

I don't think of myself as a "sick person." To me, hemophilia is more of an inconvenience. Other than that, I'm a pretty normal kid. Sure, I get frustrated once in a while. There are many times when I can't do what my friends are doing. When that happens, I concentrate on the things I *can* do. I may not be able to play football, but I can fence, swim, and golf. There are alternatives.

If you have a chronic illness, you don't have to feel different all the time. Your illness is only a small part of you, and if you learn to cope, it just becomes another aspect of your life.

R
x

Always look on the bright side. Don't dwell on your illness if you're not having a problem on any given day.
—Greg

Hemophilia Q & A

Q: What is hemophilia?

A: There are fourteen elements in the blood called factors, which help the blood to clot. Hemophilia is a condition in which one or more of these factors are either missing or not functioning properly, making it harder for the blood to clot.

Q: What causes hemophilia?

A: Hemophilia is primarily hereditary, which means it's passed down through families. Although hemophilia can occur in females, it affects males almost exclusively. Here's why: Women carry the gene for hemophilia on an X chromosome, and women have two X chromosomes, while men have one X and one Y chromosome. Most women who carry a defective X chromosome still have one healthy X chromosome, which can prevent them from developing hemophilia. Because men don't have the extra X chromosome, they may inherit *only* the defective X chromosome, causing them to develop hemophilia. There's a 50 percent chance that the son of a female carrier of hemophilia will develop it. Hemophilia can also develop through a spontaneous mutation in the genes, meaning the genes can, over generations, change form and become defective. Then hemophilia can suddenly appear in families where there is no history of it.

Q: What are the effects of hemophilia?

A: Hemophilia causes painful episodes of internal bleeding. Though this bleeding is usually in the joints and muscles, it can also take place in organs, including the brain. Bleeding in joints can cause chronic arthritis.

Q: How many people have hemophilia?

A: Worldwide, approximately 1 in every 10,000 people has hemophilia. In the U.S., health officials estimate that 17,000 people have factor VIII deficiency (also called hemophilia A); 2,800 have factor IX deficiency (also called hemophilia B); and 200 have factor VII, X, XI, or XIII deficiency.

Q: How is hemophilia treated?

A: Blood plasma containing the missing or dysfunctional factor(s) is injected into the patient. Patients can also inject themselves with a solution containing the missing or dysfunctional factor(s). Both methods help restore the blood's ability to clot.

Sources: MedAccess Corporation; National Hemophilia Foundation; World Federation of Hemophilia.

Organizations

National Hemophilia Foundation
116 West 32nd Street, 11th Floor
New York, NY 10001
1-800-42-HANDI (Information Center)
1-888-INFO-NHF (National Office)
FAX: (212) 328-3799 (Information Center)
FAX: (212) 328-3777 (National Office)
http://www.hemophilia.org

The NHF publishes a magazine *(HemAware)* and a newsletter *(Community Alert)* and offers a library of free hemophilia information. The NHF also advocates in Congress on behalf of people with hemophilia and organizes peer support programs nationwide. HANDI (Hemophilia AIDS/HIV Network for the Dissemination of Information) Center staffers can refer you to local hemophilia treatment centers and support programs.

World Federation of Hemophilia
1425 Rene-Levesque Boulevard West, Suite 1010
Montreal, Quebec H3G 1T7
Canada
(514) 875-7944
FAX: (514) 875-8916
http://www.wfh.org

Dedicated to the treatment of hemophilia around the world, this organization offers free materials—general information about hemophilia, a guide for travelers with hemophilia, and a newsletter. Its main focus, however, is on the developing world, and the Federation works with health officials worldwide to establish treatment and support programs in developing countries. Check out its Web site for links to hemophilia sites and organizations around the globe.

Web site

Hemophilia Home Page
http://www.web-depot.com/hemophilia

Maintained by Michael Davon (who has hemophilia and HIV), this site definitely has an attitude. Aside from general information, electronic mailing lists, pen pals, research news, and lots of links to other resources, the site features memorials to people who have died as a result of hemophilia and HIV. It also includes controversial items, such as news about marijuana as a treatment for pain.

Jessica
(Diabetes)

Jessica Pray is sixteen years old and a junior in high school. She is a Type I (insulin-dependent) diabetic. Jessica lives with her parents, her sister, Sara, and her stepbrothers, Mike and Chris. She is co-editor of her school yearbook and enjoys writing, hanging out with her friends, and playing volleyball. She also works part-time as a waitress. Jessica plans to attend college and eventually work in biomedical research. Her goal is to find new and better medications to help people with chronic illnesses like diabetes.

I was diagnosed with diabetes when I was thirteen. It all began when I got the flu. While I was sick, I tried to drink as many fluids as I could. I started to drink a lot of Coke, which is absolutely loaded with sugar. Weeks went by, and I was still really thirsty all of the time. I started having to urinate every half hour or so; then I was going every ten minutes, and I felt really tired. The symptoms were odd. I thought, "What kind of problem makes you have to go to the bathroom so much?" It just didn't make a lot of sense to me.

But since nothing else seemed wrong, we let it go. My mom and I considered going to the doctor, but then we'd put it off. We thought that I was just growing or that I had some kind of virus, but I kept getting worse. Finally, my mom said, "It sounds like diabetes, but that's ridiculous because no one in our family has it." At the time, we thought that you could only get diabetes if you inherited it. Actually, you *can* inherit diabetes, but you can also just develop it.

We finally went to the doctor, and when we told her about the symptoms, she agreed with my mom that I might have diabetes. That's when I started getting worried. I didn't know much about diabetes—just that it had something to do with sugar. I had to take a glucose test (where you drink a sugary solution) to measure the rate at which my body removes glucose from my blood. I waited for a half an hour in the clinic, then they tested my blood sugar to see how my body was handling the glucose. A normal person would have a glucose level of 60 to 115 milligrams per deciliter. Mine was 419 . . . just a little high, huh?

I was diagnosed with diabetes right before Halloween, and I'll never forget it. I found out that the type of diabetes I have means that my body has trouble producing insulin, a hormone that helps you metabolize carbohydrates. When I heard what was involved in treating diabetes—injecting myself twice a day with insulin, testing my blood, and monitoring my diet—I was more upset than I've ever been in my entire life. To make matters worse, I couldn't have any candy that Halloween and was stuck at home handing out candy to trick-or-treaters.

My doctor showed me how to inject the insulin. I just took a needle, filled it

Jessica *(front)* with her friend, Nicole

with some insulin, and injected it into my tissue. People usually inject a place where it's less likely to hurt (their buttocks or stomach). I didn't mind injecting myself, but having to test my blood and watch my diet seemed like a real pain. At age thirteen, the last thing I wanted was to have to figure out what I could and couldn't eat. When I realized that I now had lots of food restrictions, I was really unhappy—I knew the diabetes was going to be there constantly, forever.

Because of the diabetes, I had to test my blood to find out how much insulin my body needed. I hated to do the testing. I didn't like having to pull out the machine (a glucose monitor) for measuring my blood-sugar level. I had to prick my finger with a little needle, then squeeze a drop of blood onto a test strip, which just looks like a strip of paper. Then I'd put the paper into the machine to get a reading. You can't conceal the machine in any way, and people would look at me and say, "What in the world are you doing?" I had to test my blood a lot at first, but I eventually got the hang of knowing how much insulin I needed.

After I was diagnosed with diabetes, I stood up in front of my class and explained the disease. It was a small school that was more like a little community, so I felt comfortable getting things out in the open. I told the class the name of my disease and how I had to test my blood and give myself insulin injections. Everyone took it really well—no one was upset or anything. I was worried that people might not understand. I didn't want them to think I was contagious and be afraid to be around me. I guess I explained my illness pretty well because no one had any questions. Once in a while, people will ask me questions, but just out of curiosity, not disgust or fear.

Now if I ever have to test my blood in front of my classmates, I let them know what I'm going to do beforehand. I don't want to just whip out a needle without explaining why. I don't have a problem being honest about my illness, but sometimes I get tired of explaining. People are generally understanding about my diabetes, and they respect that I have to take care of myself.

▲▼▲▼▲▼▲▼

I had to learn a lot of nutrition information because of my disease. Diabetics are supposed to limit their intake of simple carbohydrates but eat a lot of complex carbohydrates. Simple carbohydrates come from white sugar and from foods made with white refined flour. Simple carbohydrates and sugars hit your system right away. If you eat a candy bar, for example, you have a rush of energy for about an hour, but then your sugar level drops really low. The complex carbohydrates in whole-grain products also give you energy, but they're first metabolized into glucose instead of hitting your system directly. Your body takes longer to convert complex carbohydrates into energy, so you have more of a sustained level of blood sugar. Gradually, I've learned to be able to look at foods and automatically have a pretty good idea of how many carbohydrates they contain.

During the first year after my diagnosis, I talked to a nutritionist who helped me understand and plan my diet. I also have some books at home on what I'm supposed to eat, and now it's pretty easy for me to plan my eating. Sometimes, though, it's a pain, like when I go out to eat. I have to figure out if the waiter has accidentally given me a regular soda instead of diet soda. You know how sometimes it's hard to tell? If I drink a regular soda by mistake, I'll end up getting high blood sugar.

My doctor told me that I could have a "treat night" once a week, where I was allowed to eat some candy or a piece of cake, for example. By taking more insulin when I was planning to have dessert, I could control the effects that eating sweets had on my body. But the truth is, I always have to *plan* my eating. I need to make sure that I consume a certain number of calories and eat at roughly the same times every day. I can't just indulge in a piece of cake at two o'clock in the afternoon if I feel like it. And I can't just take anything I'm offered—gum, candy, lollipops. Little things like that are off-limits. If my blood-sugar level gets too high, I start to feel really sick. I might have trouble breathing, throw up, or—if it gets really bad—go into a coma.

I had a lot of trouble adjusting to my diabetes the first year. I thought it wasn't fair that I had this disease. Even worse than not being able to indulge in sweets was the fact that I couldn't sleep late on weekends. I had to wake up by nine o'clock every morning to inject myself. When I would sleep over at someone's house and stay up until four or five A.M., I'd still have to get up at nine. Gradually, my internal clock began to wake me in time for my injection. I didn't like this routine, but it was something I had to deal with.

My mom would try to make me feel better, but that didn't help. Sometimes I'd go to bed upset and wake up the next morning feeling a little better. It just took some time. To help me adjust, my mom decided to take me to a psychologist. He told me about a support group for teens with diabetes, and I thought I would check it out. I attended a meeting and enjoyed it, so I went back again. Slowly, I got to know the people there and felt more comfortable. I began to get involved in the conversations more and more. It's a pretty nice group, and I still like going.

After I'd been attending my support group for a few months, a new girl who had just been diagnosed came to a meeting. I told her, "Even though this seems like some kind of crazy nightmare and you want to wake up, you won't. You'll have to adapt to having a disease, but over time, it will just become part of your life, automatic. And remember that it's okay to cry. Go ahead and cry for days, weeks even. Ask for pity. Feel sorry for yourself. It's only natural. But you have to move on. If you let depression be a priority in your life, you're not taking care of yourself." That's what I wish someone would have said to me.

I know that some people with chronic illnesses have a problem telling their friends and other people. They get really shy about explaining the disease and its effects. I guess I'm the kind of person who likes to share what I'm feeling, instead of trying to hide it. The way I look at it, how do you hide something so big? It's such a huge part of your life. If I had to describe myself, I'd probably talk about my physical appearance first, then say, "I'm diabetic." There's no use keeping my illness a secret.

▲▼▲▼▲▼▲▼

I feel lucky to have a wonderful doctor. We have a really good relationship. She listens to me and is always open to my suggestions. That's important to me because, as a patient, I feel that I should have a say about what's going on with my body. For example, when I learned about the insulin pump (a machine that pumps insulin into the body), I wanted to get one so that I wouldn't have to do any more injections. Using the pump is a big responsibility for a teenager, and there are some risks involved because you're relying on a machine to work properly all the time. Still, my doctor was supportive of the idea. About three years after I was diagnosed, I started using an insulin pump instead of insulin injections.

The pump looks like a pager and can clip onto my jeans or skirt, or fit right in my pocket. We're not allowed to have pagers at my school, so people will ask, "Hey, what are you doing with a pager?" Then I tell them it's my pump, and I show them how it works. A clear tube is attached to a needle at one end and to the pump at the other end; insulin is pumped through the tube into my skin where the needle is. The best way to describe the pump is to say that it's like an IV (an apparatus for intravenous injections or feeding), but instead of going into a vein, the needle just goes in my tissue. I insert the needle and tube into my abdomen, under my clothes. About every five days, I replace the insulin and change the tubing by moving it from one side of my abdomen to the other.

When I first stick the needle in, it stings for about fifteen or twenty minutes, but then I get used to it and I don't really feel it.

So far, I've had only one bad experience with my insulin pump. I was at work, and the pump was under my uniform. At some point during my waitressing shift, I must have scratched my stomach where the tube was. I went to the bathroom at the end of my shift, about four hours later, to discover that the tube had fallen out and was bent. I realized that I was having trouble breathing and that my heart was beating really fast—I thought I was going to pass out. On top of that, I couldn't find my test kit to test my blood-sugar level. (Later I discovered I'd left it at home.) I had to go to the hospital and get my blood sugar tested; it was somewhere between 500 and 600—the worst it ever was. It was scary!

In spite of this one problem, the pump has really made a difference in my life. Using an insulin pump means no more injections—it's *so much* better than shots. I can sleep in now because I don't have to wake up for an injection anymore. Although I still have to watch my diet carefully, I can usually eat what I want, when I want—it's excellent. I just have to calculate the carbohydrates I'm going to eat and then adjust the amount of insulin pumping into my body.

▲▼▲▼▲▼▲▼

Diabetes can be an overwhelming disease. I have to spend a lot of time just taking care of myself, and even when I'm not focusing on the diabetes, it's still there. Sometimes I break down and cry, and sometimes I take my anger out on my family, but I don't mean to. If I start dwelling too much on my chronic illness, I get upset and have a hard time.

Writing helps me deal with my disease. I love writing, and I'm pretty good at expressing my thoughts. I just put my feelings down on paper. I write when I'm upset in general, too. It makes me feel better to let stuff out.

I look at my friends and think that they're lucky to not have to deal with so much at such a young age. I have a lot to think about with my diabetes and treatment. Sometimes I feel like I'm one step ahead of my friends when it comes to responsibility because they don't have as much to worry about. I've been through a lot—I feel like I've had to mature faster, and I have a better grip on some things. Don't get me wrong—I'm sixteen and I definitely show that a lot, but when times are tough, I can handle myself pretty well . . . maybe better than some other people my age.

In some ways, diabetes has made me a much more responsible person. It keeps me in line. It teaches me about life. If a cure for diabetes is discovered, that would be great, but in the meantime I'm doing okay. It's just part of who I am. I've adapted.

R_X

Follow your treatment and stay positive. Having a chronic illness will just blend in, like learning to walk and everything else new in life.

—Jessica

Diabetes Q & A

Q: What is diabetes?

A: Diabetes is a chronic disorder in which the body is unable to properly convert food into energy or control its production of glucose (blood sugar). The result is a deficiency of insulin, a hormone that helps the body metabolize carbohydrates. Type I (insulin-dependent) diabetes is a disorder in which the body produces little or no insulin, while Type II (noninsulin-dependent) is a metabolic disorder in which the body is unable to produce enough insulin or properly use the insulin it produces.

Q: What causes diabetes?

A: The cause is unknown. It's thought that Type I diabetes is the result of an autoimmune disorder, which means that the immune system mistakenly thinks the body is sick and produces antibodies to fight illness. These antibodies end up attacking the body's healthy tissue. Type I diabetes may also be triggered by a viral infection. It's thought that Type II diabetes is the result of a genetic predisposition (the diabetes patient may have been born with something that caused the illness to develop). Some medications have been known to cause diabetic symptoms by impairing the secretion of insulin or causing the body to resist the effects of insulin. The diabetic symptoms usually disappear shortly after the medication works its way out of the patient's system.

Q: What are the effects of diabetes?

A: Diabetes can cause hypoglycemia (low blood sugar) by producing too much insulin and hyperglycemia (high blood sugar) by producing too little insulin. High and low blood sugar can, in many cases, produce similar symptoms, including irritability, unusual mood change, rapid speech, confusion, dizziness, poor coordination, headache, blurred vision, and weakness. High levels of glucose in the blood over many years can cause damage to organs. High blood sugar also increases the chance of heart and blood vessel disease. If high or low blood sugar is untreated, the diabetes patient may have a seizure and eventually lapse into a coma.

Q: How many people have diabetes?

A: Between 12 and 15 million people in the U.S. have diabetes. Approximately 10 percent of patients have Type I diabetes, and the remaining 90 percent have Type II. Of the 650,000 cases of diabetes diagnosed each year, 13,000 are people 18 and under.

Q: How is diabetes treated?

A: Diabetes is most commonly treated with insulin injections. People who have diabetes can learn to test their blood-sugar level, administer insulin injections, and/or choose snacks that can help regulate their glucose level. Diabetics must regulate their diet to achieve a balance between carbohydrates, sugar, fat, and protein. They are also encouraged to maintain a healthy weight and exercise regularly. Some medications can curb the effects of diabetes.

Sources: American Diabetes Association; *The Essential Guide to Chronic Illness* by James W. Long, M.D. (NY: HarperCollins, 1997).

Diabetes Resources

Organizations

American Diabetes Association
1660 Duke Street
Alexandria, VA 22314
1-800-232-3472
FAX: (703) 549-6995
http://www.diabetes.org

Dedicated to diabetes education and awareness, the ADA has lots of free information on screening, treatment, nutrition, support groups, research, and legislative issues. The ADA Web site features diabetes information and an online store.

Juvenile Diabetes Foundation
120 Wall Street
New York, NY 10005
1-800-223-1138
(212) 785-9500
FAX: (212) 785-9595
http://www.jdfcure.com

Dedicated to finding a cure and treatments for diabetes and to promoting diabetes education, the JDF is a great source of free information. Staff members can put you in touch with your local JDF chapter where you can get physician referrals and support group information.

National Diabetes Information Clearinghouse
One Information Way
Bethesda, MD 20892-3560
(301) 654-3327
FAX: (301) 907-8900
http://www.niddk.nih.gov/health/diabetes/ndic.htm

Sponsored by the National Institutes of Health, this organization provides general informational materials (most are free of charge) about diabetes. The Web site has information on treatments, research, nutrition, and more. For a list of documents you can read online or download, go to: *http://www.niddk.nih.gov/health/diabetes/diabetes.htm*

Books

Diabetes 101: A Pure and Simple Guide for People Who Use Insulin by Betty Page Brackenridge, M.S., R.D., C.D.E., and Richard O. Dolinar, M.D. (Minnetonka, MN: Chronimed Publishing, 1998). Learn along with Mike, a young man with diabetes, as he visits his doctor and diabetes educator and receives practical advice on controlling his diabetes. This useful book offers information on monitoring blood sugar, nutrition, exercise, and dealing with common illnesses.

Living with Diabetes: A Comprehensive Guide to Understanding and Controlling Diabetes While Enjoying Your Life by Arlan L. Rosenbloom, M.D., and Diana Tonnessen (NY: Plume, 1993). The authors of this general guide to living with diabetes want to empower readers to manage their illness. The book includes information about the diagnosis and treatment of diabetes, along with tips on how to control diabetes complications. Also includes a list of resources and recipes.

Web site

Diabetes.com
http://www.diabetes.com

Sponsored by NetHealth, an Internet guide to health-oriented Web sites, this site includes the latest diabetes news, information on support groups and research, an online bookstore, and lots of links to other resources on the Internet. You can post a message on the site's bulletin board or enter the kids' section for information on summer camps for young people with diabetes.

Rachel
(Epilepsy)

Rachel Brummel is an eighteen-year-old high school senior. She has epilepsy, a disorder of the electrical impulses in the brain, which periodically causes attacks called seizures. Rachel has three brothers—two older and one younger. She enjoys playing sports, especially softball and volleyball, and runs both indoor and outdoor track. She's also active in her school's speech club. Rachel is thinking about attending college in Maryland, possibly the University of Maryland, Mount Saint Mary's, or Towson State University. She hasn't yet decided what she'll study, but she's interested in early childhood education, broadcasting, and neurology (the study of the brain and its functions).

One morning when I was nine years old, I didn't get out of bed. At the time, no one knew what had happened, but it turned out that I'd had a seizure and was sick to my stomach; the seizure caused me to fall into a deep sleep. When my mom came into my room and tried to wake me up, I didn't respond. Then my younger brother, Peter, came in and tried to talk to me, but I didn't respond to him, either. My mom called a neighbor and asked her to come over. They all tried to talk to me, but no one could get through. Finally, my mom called an ambulance, and I was taken to the hospital.

At the hospital, the doctors ran all kinds of tests to figure out what was wrong. The doctors finally performed a CAT scan, a test that shows brain activity. The CAT scan revealed activity related to a seizure, and as a result, I was diagnosed with epilepsy.

I was really surprised by the diagnosis. Although I'd heard of epilepsy once or twice, I didn't know anything about it. I was confused because the doctor never sat down and explained things to me. He just glossed over everything, saying that epilepsy was a brain disorder; that's all I was told.

Rachel at Halloween

I never developed much of a relationship with that doctor. He wasn't very good at communicating with me and helping me get involved in making decisions about my treatment. I didn't even know that I had the option to make these kinds of decisions. I didn't realize that I had a say in my own treatment.

▲▼▲▼▲▼▲▼

After my diagnosis, I left the hospital without a clear understanding of what seizures were, let alone how they would affect my life. I had this terrible fear that the epilepsy was going to slowly eat away at my brain. I suddenly felt different from everyone. I was afraid that other people would think I was different, too. I was so scared that they'd think I was weird and wouldn't treat me the same anymore.

Now I know that there are basically four kinds of seizures—grand mal, petit mal, complex partial, and simple partial. Grand mal seizures are the worst kind, characterized by jerking movements. These seizures usually last for just a few minutes, but they can leave you feeling sleepy, fatigued, and confused for hours (the seizure I had at age nine was a grand mal). Petit mal seizures aren't as severe and usually last only a few seconds. If you're having a petit mal seizure, you might appear to be daydreaming and have a blank look on your face. Complex partial seizures can also make you look like you're in a trance; these seizures can cause uncontrolled body movements, such as walking around aimlessly or suddenly striking out at things. A lot of times complex partial seizures begin with strange sensations like fear, nausea, or hallucinations. The fourth kind of seizure is simple partial. Things can suddenly look strange if you're having the seizure—you might see people or things that aren't really there. You may also have odd sensations on one side of your body.

At first, my seizures were mild, and they mostly just made me blank out or feel fuzzy and disoriented—they weren't violent or anything. Because the seizures weren't affecting me very much, my doctor explained that he didn't think it was a good idea for me to take medications to try to control them. Many drugs used to treat epilepsy can cause side effects like drowsiness; some can dull your personality or mute your emotions.

Most of my seizures were complex partial, which made me feel really weird, like I was in a dream—it was as if I was being lifted outside of my body. The feeling would wear off after a few minutes, but I'd still feel strange and really out of it afterwards. Sometimes I'd also feel nauseated and tired, get headaches, and have to go to the bathroom.

I started having more grand mal seizures a few years after my diagnosis, and these seizures were awful because of the jerking movements. At the time, I was eleven and we had just moved from Minnesota to Maryland. We found a doctor at the University of

Maryland Medical Center who we really liked—Dr. Scheller. He was the first doctor I was able to establish a good relationship with. He took the time to explain what epilepsy is and how it works. He answered all of my questions, and for the first time I felt like I had a say in my treatment. Dr. Scheller actually cared about me, and I gradually became more comfortable with myself and my epilepsy.

As my seizures worsened, I got really sick of having them. I talked to Dr. Scheller, and we agreed that it was time to try medication. Different medications work for different people, so we knew that finding the right one for me would be a process of trial and error. We tried several medications, none of which worked very well. Each time I'd get my hopes up that the new medication would stop my seizures, but nothing seemed to work.

A few years later, we still hadn't found a successful drug. Dr. Scheller left for another hospital, and my family and I were upset because we'd been really happy with his care. He was always so nice to me and answered all of my questions. I knew that he was doing his best to find the right treatment for me.

I was lucky to find another good doctor, Dr. Koch. He's still trying different medications with me because we haven't found one that effectively prevents all of my seizures. In all, I've tried five or six different kinds of medication. We'll keep looking until we find the right one, but it's a frustrating process. Sometimes I feel fed up and wish Dr. Koch could just *know* what medication will work for me. But epilepsy is still a mystery in many ways, and doctors don't yet know which drugs will be successful for their particular patients.

▲▼▲▼▲▼▲▼

Because my seizures are pretty cyclical, I have an idea of the days when they're most likely to happen. At first, my mom and I thought that the seizures might correspond to my menstrual cycle, but my doctor hasn't been able to find evidence that they're related to *any* cycle in my body. All we know is that they happen about every forty-five days.

There are about two to four days a month when I'm more likely to have seizures. The first or second day is always the worst. I may have six to eight seizures the first day, three or four the second day, and then one or two the last couple of days. When I know the seizures are coming, I start to feel anxious and depressed. Even though I dread them, I know that I'll get through the seizures like I always do. After they're over, I gradually recover, emotionally and physically. It helps to talk to my parents—they're always very supportive.

My mom keeps a close eye on me when it's time for me to start having seizures. It helps to know that she's concerned, but I still hate having to face the fact that I'll soon be suffering through another spell of seizures. I always tell my parents when I'm not feeling well and if I've had a seizure. They're really good about letting me stay home from school when I need to; I know I can count on them to understand. My epilepsy may have actually helped us grow a little closer.

When it comes to my epilepsy, I don't really talk to my brothers (Max, 24; Ben, 21; and Peter, 14). I think Peter has a pretty good understanding of what epilepsy is, but he still gets upset when I have grand mal seizures. I think everyone in my family gets frustrated now and then because we don't have any control over the epilepsy. None of us can do anything to prevent my seizures.

▲▼▲▼▲▼▲▼

I had a horrible experience last year, toward the end of a school day. It was during one of my seizure spells, and I'd had some smaller seizures earlier in the day. I thought that maybe I wouldn't have any more that day because I'd been feeling somewhat better.

I was walking down the hall when suddenly—out of nowhere—this awful feeling rose up through my body. I couldn't stop it, and the feeling just kept spreading. Then I felt tired and dazed, and everything became a blur. Later, I woke up in the nurse's office with a bump on my head and a huge headache. I'd had a grand mal seizure.

It's pretty embarrassing to have a seizure at school. Once in a while, people will ask me about the seizures, but most kids I know don't ask anything about my epilepsy at all. One time, a girl in my journalism class said, "Um, Rachel, I heard you had a seizure. Are you okay?" I totally shrugged it off and said, "Yeah, I'm fine," and completely dropped the subject. I don't really like to talk about my epilepsy with people I'm not close to.

I know that I'm able to get beyond these experiences, but can other people? Epilepsy is just a tiny part of my life. I want other people to look at my epilepsy that way, too. I hope they can see me as a whole person, not just as someone with epilepsy. For a long time, I never even talked to my friends about my health problems. I was afraid they'd no longer see me as the same person they'd always known.

Just a few months ago, I finally found the courage to tell my closest friends about my epilepsy. I'm sure they knew because of the seizures I've had at school, but they never said anything about it. I didn't want them to treat me any differently than they always had, but I knew that at some point I had to be honest. I wanted my close friends to know the truth, but I had to figure out a way to tell them.

The more I thought about how to tell them, the more I realized that I should just come right out and say it. I finally did, and my friends were really supportive. They said it was okay and assured me that they still thought of me as the same person they'd always known. Opening up hasn't changed any of my friendships for the worse, and I'm really relieved that I was honest. I feel like a big weight has been lifted from my shoulders, and I don't have to worry anymore.

My teachers know about my epilepsy, too, because of the chance that I'll have a seizure in one of their classes. The school nurse and I worked together to write a letter to my teachers, explaining that I have epilepsy and offering instructions for what to do if I have a grand mal seizure during class. Aside from the actual seizures, my epilepsy hasn't caused problems for me at school. My teachers are understanding, and the nurse is always helpful, too.

▲ ▼▲ ▼▲ ▼▲ ▼

I think that the worst part of having epilepsy is the overwhelming power and unfair timing it seems to have. One day I'll feel great— like I'm on top of the world. Then, that same night, I'll have a seizure and come crashing down. I'll be forced to let everything else go and just give in to the seizures, which wear my body down physically. It's exhausting, and I usually feel nauseated and have a splitting headache afterward. Mentally, I'll be forgetful and disoriented, and emotionally, I'll be left with overwhelming feelings of sadness and anger. These feelings generally wear off within a few hours of the seizure.

Epilepsy can cause a lot of suffering. You're not in control, the grand mal seizures can be really hard on your body, and you have to deal with people's ignorance. Coping with my epilepsy has helped me to be more sensitive to the physical and emotional problems of others. I understand what it's like to be sick or depressed, and I can really empathize. I think my epilepsy has made me more considerate of other people in general.

Having an illness like this has also made me more appreciative of good health. Young people often tend to take their health for granted, thinking doctors and hospitals are for old people. I've definitely learned to appreciate the times when I'm feeling good and am not troubled with seizures. I'm an active person and enjoy playing sports, so I try to make the most of the days when I feel good.

My advice to other young people who have health issues is to get the facts about your illness. Learn about it. Find out what causes it and how it can be treated. If you don't understand what you're dealing with, you can't play an active role or make good decisions about your treatment. Talk to your doctor. Ask questions. Keep in mind that different things work for different people. Don't be depressed if your treatment doesn't work. Talk to your doctor and try something else.

Life with a chronic illness is hard, but you'll get through it. There will be difficult times, and you'll deal with them. It really helps to talk to people about your feelings. After a rough spot is over, you'll begin to feel better. You may have another challenge to face, but you'll face it and move on. There's always tomorrow, and tomorrow will be better.

R_X

You're definitely not alone. There are lots of people out there who have a chronic illness or all kinds of other health issues. Don't give up!

—Rachel

Epilepsy Q & A

Q: What is epilepsy?

A: Epilepsy is a neurological disorder that causes brief disturbances in the electrical functions of the brain. Millions of electrical charges pass from nerve cells in the brain to all parts of the body; with epilepsy, electrical activity is disrupted by sudden bursts that are much stronger than the normal electrical flow.

Q: What causes epilepsy?

A: Many people with epilepsy may have been born with the conditions that cause it. For example, during birth, a lack of oxygen for the baby might cause damage to the brain. Epileptic conditions may also develop later in life as a result of injury, infections, abnormalities in the structure of the brain, or exposure to toxic agents. There may be other causes of epilepsy that haven't yet been discovered.

Q: What are the effects of epilepsy?

A: These bursts of electrical energy may cause the patient to lose consciousness or to have a seizure. Seizures are a symptom of epilepsy, but not everyone who has had a seizure necessarily has epilepsy. Some illnesses or severe injuries can affect the body enough to produce a single seizure. However, epilepsy is a permanent condition that affects the brain's ability to regulate its electrical activity, causing recurring seizures.

Q: How many people have epilepsy?

A: Approximately 1 percent of the U.S. population—more than two million people. Epilepsy can develop at any time of life, and approximately 125,000 cases are diagnosed each year. One-third of these cases are children.

Q: How is epilepsy treated?

A: The three most common forms of treatment are drugs, surgery, or a special diet. Drug therapy is the most common treatment, and a number of medications are designed to treat various types of seizures. Surgery may be performed if the epilepsy is caused by a tumor in the brain or if medication fails to control the seizures. The diet used to treat epilepsy is called a ketogenic diet (it's high in fats and low in carbohydrates, which produces an excess of a compound called ketone). The extra ketone creates a chemical condition in the body called ketosis, which prevents seizures in some people. As with surgery, a ketogenic diet is used only when medication is unsuccessful. While it has a higher success rate in children, the ketogenic diet doesn't work in the majority of patients with epilepsy.

Source: Epilepsy Foundation of America.

Epilepsy Resources

Organizations

Epilepsy Foundation of America
4351 Garden City Drive
Landover, MD 20785
1-800-EFA-1000 (Information and referral line)
1-800-332-4050 (Information library)
1-800-213-5821 (Catalog sales)
(301) 459-3700
FAX: (301) 577-2684
http://www.efa.org

The EFA is dedicated to educating the public about epilepsy and has a huge amount of free information; staffers can send you brochures and fact sheets and refer you to clinics and treatment centers in your area. You can also have specific questions answered over the phone by calling the information library. The EFA Web site has an online bookstore, a bulletin board where you can post messages, and a special "Kid's Club" especially for young children that includes useful information for people of all ages.

Wake Forest University School of Medicine Epilepsy Information Service
Medical Center Boulevard
Winston-Salem, NC 27157-1078
1-800-642-0500
FAX: (336) 716-9489
http://www.bgsm.edu/PatientCare/leadingservices/inv_neuro.shtml

This service will send out free brochures and information packets based on your individual needs. Staffers can also make referrals to treatment centers and resources in your area.

Web site

People with Epilepsy
http://www.o-c-s.com/epilepsy

This nonprofit organization is dedicated to educating the public about epilepsy. The Web site includes general epilepsy information, chat rooms, mailing lists, book reviews, articles, poetry by people with epilepsy, and research and treatment news. The site also has a section for kids with epilepsy and provides links to other resources and to personal home pages of people with epilepsy.

Carl
(Asthma)

Carl Nnoka is thirteen years old and has asthma, a condition that causes res-
piratory attacks (breathing difficulties). He lives with his mother, who founded
and coordinates a support group for parents of children with asthma. Carl is
active in Boy Scouts, and he enjoys playing baseball and hanging out with his
friends. He plans to continue his education after high school. Although he's
keeping his options open, Carl is considering becoming a naval aviator.

I found out that I have asthma about ten years ago, when I was
three. I don't actually remember how sick I used to get when I
had an asthma flare-up since I was so young then, but I know
what the attacks are like now. They can be really scary because they
narrow my air passages, making it hard to breathe. When an asthma
attack happens, I feel like I'm suffocating—like I could die.

The treatment for my asthma was much more aggressive when
I was younger. I had to go the doctor a lot and took more medication than I do now. I also used an inhaler to open my airways. An
inhaler is a little canister of medication; when you inhale from the
canister, the medication comes out in a mist that gets pulled into
your lungs. I used a nebulizer, too, which is a machine that works
sort of like an inhaler. With a nebulizer, you have to wear a mask

over your nose and mouth and inhale the medication. It's a stronger treatment than an inhaler.

As I've grown up, I haven't had as many problems with my asthma, so the treatments have been simpler. For example, by the time I was seven, I didn't have to nebulize anymore and just used my inhaler. I also started getting allergy shots once a week. (Sometimes an allergic reaction to certain foods, plant pollens, or mold would cause me to have an asthma attack.) After a couple of years, I noticed that the shots were really helping.

It's kind of funny because, even though my asthma seemed to get better after I turned seven, that was the time when it really began to interfere with my life. I'd started playing baseball and soccer, and becoming more active in general; these activities tended to aggravate my asthma attacks. I suddenly realized that I'd have to deal with my asthma every day of my life.

▲▼▲▼▲▼▲▼

I've been going to the same doctor ever since I was little, so he and I are really close. I can talk to him about my treatment, and he always listens to me. My doctor really cares about me as a person; I'm not just some kid with asthma to him. He's interested in my

life—things like my family, school, and sports—and he tells me that we'll find a way for me to do whatever I want, despite my asthma.

Whenever I've told my doctor that I've been having

Carl relaxing at home

problems with sports or because of a virus, he's been open to changing my medication. For a while, I was on a bunch of different inhalers at once, and I felt that I was using too many. When I asked if I could ease up on the medication, my doctor understood why and he let me decrease it slowly. I feel like I can help make decisions about what's best for me—having a good relationship with my doctor makes handling my asthma so much easier.

Since fourth grade, I've been taking my medication on my own. To help me, my mom made a chart on the refrigerator showing each kind of medication and when I had to take it; I had to check off the box next to the medication to show that I'd taken the dose. I learned to take the right medication at the right time, and I got used to the responsibility. After about a year, I didn't have to refer to the chart anymore because I could automatically remember what I needed to do. Now I take all of my medication when I get up in the morning and before I go to bed at night (every once in a while, I'll forget—that's when my mom starts nagging me!).

I also wear a Medic Alert necklace every day; it warns people that I have asthma, in case I can't tell them during an emergency. The necklace is hidden under my shirt so no one sees it. I know that other people wear Medic Alert necklaces and bracelets, so I don't feel weird about it.

My asthma is there every day—it's a part of me, and I just deal with it. For example, when I play baseball, I have some extra things to do to get ready for a game. I take extra medication and use a Ventolin inhaler to open up my airways. This way, I'll have more endurance during the game and will be able to run longer and faster without pain in my chest or breathing problems.

I also make sure to carry Epi Pen with me wherever I go. Epi Pen is a shot of fast-acting medication that helps the muscles in my bronchial tubes relax so my breathing passages can open up. I know that I might have to give myself a shot if I were to eat something that I'm allergic to (raw tomatoes or nuts can make me have a severe asthma attack). Even though I get regular allergy shots, I still have some allergies to foods and I always need to be prepared. If the allergic reaction is really severe, I might need oxygen, nebulizer treatments, or a trip to the hospital. I'm not worried about it, though, because I have my Epi Pen and I know what to do. These are adjustments that I've made in my life because of my asthma.

▲▼▲▼▲▼▲▼

Every year, my mom talks to the nurse and teachers at my school about my asthma so they understand what I can and can't do. My physical education teachers know that I'll at least try to do as many activities as possible, but sometimes I'll need to sit out and just watch for a while. Other kids have to sit out for different reasons (like injuries), so it's not as if I'm the only one. As a safety precaution, we told my baseball coach that I have asthma because he has to know what to do if I have an attack during a game. Although I can do almost everything that other kids can do, I have to make sure that the people in charge understand my condition and know how to help me if I have problems.

For the third summer in a row, I'm going away to camp for three weeks, and I have to take a bunch of instructions for the counselors and the nurse so they know about my asthma and medication schedule. The instructions also explain what to do if I have an asthma attack and where to contact my mom. Before I go to camp each year, my mom stocks up on extra inhalers and medications to make sure I have enough to last for the whole time I'm away from home. She usually gets way too many—more than I could use in two months!

I feel fortunate that my mom knows so much about asthma, and I'm really proud of her work with her support group. She started the group herself ten years ago because people needed one, and she helps a lot of parents and their kids. Her experience makes me feel really safe—I know that if anything happens to me, she'll know what to do and I'll be okay.

I had never paid much attention to my mom's asthma support group until a couple of years ago, when I heard her talking to someone about it. I asked her to tell me about what kind of work she did there. After she explained that she helps parents and their kids cope with asthma, I became more interested in how the meetings worked. I went to a few of them and talked to other kids who have asthma. I realized that many of them were having a lot of trouble dealing with their treatments and were upset about taking medication. I thought maybe I could help them feel better, so I told them about how they'll eventually get used to their asthma like I did. I said that other kids at school usually don't make a big deal about treatments unless you do.

One time, we were at a beach in North Carolina with one of my mom's friends from the support group. Her friend brought her two sons along. One of the boys has asthma but had never used a peak-flow meter, an instrument that measures air flow from your lungs. I knew how a peak-flow meter worked because I'd used one to monitor my asthma in the past. Because he seemed really afraid to use the instrument, I showed him how to do it, and he felt much more comfortable about the whole thing. I was really glad that I could help.

Helping other kids accept their asthma makes me feel good about myself. It's neat to know that just by setting an example, I can be someone's inspiration. That's one of the good things about having a chronic illness—the chance it gives you to do something good for others.

▲▽▲▽▲▽▲▽

Of course, there are always difficult things to face when you have a chronic illness. For example, if you have asthma, you may also have to deal with food allergies. This can be really rough—especially when you eat out with friends—and you have to find creative ways to work around your allergies. Well, so what if you can't eat milk chocolate or other foods? I know kids who can't eat cake and other stuff with milk in it, so their moms make them Rice Krispies treats. There are so many other things you *can* eat—you can always find solutions.

I don't think I'm that different from my friends, and my friends don't act like I am. I can usually do everything they do and have just as much fun. But one difference between us is that I'm more aware of other people who have health problems. One year, there was a girl with arthritis in our class.* The teacher told us not to help the girl because, even though movement was painful for her, it was better for her arthritis. I'd feel upset when I'd see the girl hurting, and I'd always want to help her even though I knew that I couldn't. Maybe I understood her since I have a chronic illness, too.

There are times when I do feel different in a not-so-good way. For me, it usually happens when I have to carry my medications around with me. They're all in a little canvas pouch, and if people ask me about what's inside of it, I feel self-conscious because I don't want them to wonder if I'm sick. Because asthma isn't an everyday illness like a cold, I'm afraid people will think I'm weird. I'm sure it's normal for kids with chronic illnesses to worry about what other people think of them.

Sometimes it's been really frustrating to have a chronic illness. When I was in elementary school, we had a physical fitness test that involved different activities and events. I did really well on most parts of the test and even got some of the highest scores in the class. But when it was time to run the mile, I couldn't do nearly as well as the others kids because my asthma held me back. That one event kept me from getting the fitness award, which was hard for me to deal with. Then I realized that I can accomplish lots of other things in my life. I know now that it's a waste of time to focus only on my limitations.

Although you may have many difficult things to deal with, life with a chronic illness can still be okay. I've learned that lesson lots of times. Don't let your chronic illness keep you from succeeding. You may not be able to do things the way you thought you would, but in the end, you can still reach your goals.

*For more on arthritis, see pp. 84–93.

R_X

When you have a chronic illness, you just have to go a different way. There are always alternatives to choose from. You can still live your life and be happy.

—Carl

Asthma Q & A

Q: What is asthma?

A: Asthma is a "reactive airway" disease that causes breathing difficulties, inflamed airways, and sensitivity to different triggers such as cigarette smoke, colds, and food allergies.

Q: What causes asthma?

A: The basic cause of the lung abnormality in asthma isn't yet known, but asthma can be triggered by allergies to certain foods or irritants such as pollen, smoke, air pollution, and animal dander. It can also be caused by respiratory problems like chronic bronchitis and emphysema. Asthma is often triggered by heavy or labored breathing, which can result from physical activity, hard laughter, fear, or nervousness.

Q: What are the effects of asthma?

A: Asthma causes the muscles in the walls of the bronchial tubes (airways) to tighten during heavy breathing, which causes production of excess mucus. The combination of these two factors results in the narrowing of the air passageway, reducing air flow. This causes breathing difficulty, coughing, and wheezing. While asthmatics have no trouble inhaling large breaths, they can have great difficulty exhaling; this is what causes the wheezing sound of asthma attacks. Severe asthma may be accompanied by sweating, insomnia, and a bluish discoloration of the face and extremities (fingers, toes).

Q: How many people have asthma?

A: About 4.8 million young people (under 18) have asthma. It's the most common serious illness among children and, of all chronic illnesses, causes the most lost schooldays per year (10 million).

Q: How is asthma treated?

A: Several medications are available to reduce the chance of an asthma attack and to open the airways once an attack begins. Some of these medications are administered by inhalers (devices that spray a mist of the medication into the lungs). Other medication can be taken in the form of pills. Asthma patients may work with respiratory therapists to learn breathing techniques or may receive shots to curb allergic reactions.

Sources: American Academy of Pediatrics; American Lung Association; *The Essential Guide to Chronic Illness* by James W. Long, M.D. (NY: HarperCollins, 1997).

Organizations

Allergy and Asthma Network/Mothers of Asthmatics, Inc.
2751 Prosperity Avenue, Suite 150
Fairfax, VA 22031
1-800-878-4403
(703) 641-9595
FAX: (703) 573-7794
http://www.aanma.org/

This organization—dedicated to patient education—provides brochures, books, and videos on the latest medical news, treatments, asthma and allergy products, and health-care legislation.

Allergy/Asthma Information Association
130 Bridgeland Avenue, Suite 424
Toronto, Ontario M6A 1Z4
Canada
1-800-611-7011
(416) 783-8944
FAX: (416) 783-7538

This group offers free information on asthma and allergies for patients, families, and doctors, plus provides over-the-phone support and referrals to physicians in your area.

American Lung Association
1740 Broadway
New York, NY 10019
1-800-LUNG-USA
http://www.lungusa.org

This large organization provides brochures, pamphlets, and videos on lung and breathing diseases and has excellent resources for young people and families.

Asthma and Allergy Foundation of America
1125 15th Street, NW, Suite 502
Washington, DC 20005
1-800-7-ASTHMA (Information line)
(202) 466-7643 (Main office)
FAX: (202) 466-8940
http://www.aafa.org

Dedicated to finding a cure, the Foundation supports research, educates the public, and advocates for people with asthma and allergies. The AAFA offers free brochures and information on asthma and allergy research, medications, support groups, and products. The AAFA also organizes SAY (Support for Asthmatic Youth) and Pals, a pen-pal program for young people with asthma and allergies.

Books

American Lung Association Family Guide to Asthma and Allergies by American Lung Association Asthma Advisory Group (Boston, MA: Little Brown & Company, 1998). You'll find lots of practical information in this comprehensive guide for families with asthma and allergies. The book contains helpful tips for making life easier at home and school.

Living with Asthma: A Comprehensive Guide to Understanding and Controlling Your Asthma While Enjoying Your Life by Anthony Rooklin, M.D., and Shelagh Ryan Masling (NY: Plume, 1995). This easy-to-read book has lots of information on symptoms and treatments, as well as advice for living with asthma; it also includes chapters on exercise and controlling environmental factors that trigger breathing difficulties.

Web site

Allergy & Asthma Web Site
http://www.allernet.com

This useful Web site provides answers to frequently asked questions, links to other organizations, an online newsletter, and lists of asthma and allergy specialists around the United States. Check out the site's allergy forecast maps, which show pollen and mold-spore levels across the U.S.

Kristy

(Cancer)

Kristy Sellers is an eighteen-year-old college freshman. She was diagnosed with leukemia, a form of cancer, at the age of fourteen. Kristy lives with her parents and commutes to Hood College in Maryland, where she's double majoring in social work and sociology. She has an older brother, Eric, and enjoys public speaking, writing, swimming, horseback riding, and hanging out with her friends. She also does volunteer work for a number of organizations. Kristy hopes to enroll in graduate school at the University of Maryland, where she wants to specialize in pediatric clinical social work.

When I was a freshman in high school, things were going pretty well. I was a cheerleader and had a boyfriend. My life seemed great. Then all of a sudden, everything changed. It started with flu-like symptoms, including low-grade fevers. These symptoms went on for about two weeks, so my parents and I decided that I should see a doctor. She concluded that I had a sinus infection and gave me some medication to treat it.

But the symptoms didn't go away. I began to feel really fatigued; sometimes just walking up a flight of stairs would wipe me out, and I'd have to sit down when I reached the top of the steps. We went back to the doctor, and he said I must have anemia, a condition in which the blood is unable to carry enough oxygen throughout the body. In many cases, anemia can be cured easily, so I didn't feel too worried. I had blood drawn to confirm the diagnosis, but when the doctors examined it they saw that I had an extremely high number of white blood cells. White blood cells fight infection, and when you have a lot of them, it means your body is fighting something. The doctors decided to run some more tests.

On February 17, 1994, we went to find out the test results. The doctor called my parents into his office while I waited outside. I knew something was seriously wrong when my dad came out and was crying. I had never seen him cry before and, to be honest, it scared the hell out of me. The doctor had told my parents that I have leukemia.

The first thing I thought when I heard the news was, "Oh my god, I'm going to lose my hair." That may sound strange, but at the time, that's what my first concern was. Then I started thinking that I was going to die. I felt more scared than I'd ever been in my whole life.

The diagnosis hit my entire family really hard. It was an extremely emotional time for us, and we were all in shock. My parents asked me if I wanted to know everything about the treatment I'd have to undergo. I told

Kristy dressed up for prom

them that, good or bad, I wanted to know the whole story. I was determined to be actively involved in my treatment so I could make informed decisions.

My family is really close, and my parents wanted to be honest with me. They explained that cancer treatment is usually very hard on the body and can cause a lot of emotional ups and downs. My parents let me know that I had a right to make my own decisions about my treatment and that they would respect my choices, even when they disagreed. They promised me that they would be there for me every step of the way. There's a lot of trust in my family— that's one of the things that has helped me get through all of this.

▲▼▲▼▲▼▲▼

I began chemotherapy treatments, which consisted of injecting my body with strong chemicals in the hope that they would kill the cancer cells. Chemotherapy can cause terrible side effects, such as nausea and vomiting, fatigue, and hair loss. I got a lot of migraines (really intense headaches), and my doctors found that high doses of caffeine could help relieve them.

Early on in my treatment, I had to decide whether I wanted a catheter. There are several kinds of catheters, but in this case, it was a tube that would remain in a vein in my chest. That way, chemotherapy medications could be administered right into the catheter instead of into a vein (it can be hard to find a vein each time). It was difficult for me to decide whether to have a catheter because there are disadvantages to them. For example, I love to swim, but when you have a catheter, there's a chance it could fall out or get chlorine in it while you're in the pool. On the other hand, I wouldn't have to deal with needles going into my veins during each treatment.

At first, I decided not to get a catheter, even though my parents wanted me to. They didn't force me, and they respected my wishes. As it turned out, I have really small veins and every time I went in for treatments, the nurse had to try several times to insert the needle. In the end, I opted to get the catheter after all.

Chemotherapy really took its toll on me. The caffeine treatments for my migraines interacted with the lining of my brain, and the result was two grand mal seizures, the worst kinds of seizures you can have.* Often, people who suffer from seizures are unconscious when they happen, but I was wide awake, and it was so scary. I was lying on my hospital bed when my muscles suddenly started to contract—my arms and legs were moving uncontrollably all over the place. I was fully aware of what was going on, but I had no control over my body. My mom was there, and she started yelling and crying. Nurses rushed around the room shouting to each other.

My whole family was affected by the seizures. My dad rushed to the hospital from work, and we called my brother, who's in the Air Force. He was so upset that his commander had to drive him to the hospital to see me. I spent two days in the intensive care unit, a section of the hospital where patients with serious conditions are closely monitored.

After the seizures, I was taken for a CAT scan—a test that shows your brain activity. Normally no one, not even a parent, is allowed to be in the room while a CAT scan is conducted. My father just said to the doctors, "That's too bad," and went in anyway because he'd promised me that I'd never be alone. I was unconscious through the whole thing, but apparently when he came in, I looked up at him and started to cry.

After a month of chemotherapy, I went into remission—a period during which the cancer wasn't active. The doctors did a routine blood test to check my progress, but this time they found something new—the Philadelphia chromosome. It's so rare that only 2 percent of all kids with leukemia have it. The Philadelphia

---

*For more on seizures, see pp. 32–43.

chromosome can't be killed. No matter how many treatments you have or how long you're in remission, the cancer will at some point return. I found out that I'd most likely have to go through a cycle of remission, relapse, and more chemotherapy. It was a roller-coaster ride—first good news, then suddenly the worst news imaginable.

Chemotherapy is so hard on your body that there's only so much you can take before your body just gives out. There was only one way I could be cured—a bone marrow transplant. Bone marrow is a tissue in the cavities of most bones; in people with leukemia, the abnormal cancer cells overpopulate the bone marrow and eventually spill into the bloodstream. The healthy marrow cells can't grow properly, and this interferes with the body's normal functioning. The goal of a bone marrow transplant is to replace the cancerous bone marrow with healthy marrow.

I continued to receive chemotherapy while my doctors started the search for a bone marrow donor. Marrow is similar to blood in that not everyone's marrow type is compatible—it's much harder to find a marrow donor than a blood donor, though. There are five categories in which marrow can match. In order for a donor to be compatible, the donor's marrow needs to match that of the person with leukemia in at least three of the five categories.

There are three tiers of potential donors. The best donors are biological siblings. Because they have genes from the same two parents, it's possible for a brother or sister to be a total match. However, even though siblings have the same genes, there's only a 20 percent chance that they'll be a match. The second best candidates are nonrelated people from a list of potential donors. Profiles of volunteer donors are kept on a national database, which doctors can search for a match when someone needs a transplant. These nonrelated donors can have genetic characteristics similar enough to the patient to be better than half a match. The third donor category is the parents; they're the last choice because each of them has just half of the patient's genes. When you consider all of this, it's easy to see how difficult it can be to find a bone marrow donor.

In the search for a donor for me, my doctors started with my brother, Eric. We were really nervous because he was our best shot at finding a donor.

▲▼▲▼▲▼▲▼

While all of this was going on, I had to manage the changes leukemia was causing in the rest of my life. I lost my hair from the chemotherapy, and I had to take steroids to boost my immune system, which ended up making me gain a lot of weight. I wasn't supposed to work out because it was too much of a strain on my body, so my weight kept increasing. I was up to 202 pounds, my whole body was swollen, and I had to wear a wig. When I walked down the halls at school, guys would call me "Roseanne." Some days I just went home and cried.

My parents and brother were extremely supportive through the whole experience. I feel really fortunate to have such a great family. They cheered me up and encouraged me to keep a positive attitude. On the worst days, when I was really depressed and fatalistic, they told me that I should never give up, that I had to keep fighting.

My friends Kathy and Sabrina were great, too, and I could talk to them about everything I was going through. They were two of the few people I let see me without my wig. I didn't want to go to other friends' houses to sleep over because I knew that at some point I'd have to take off my wig. I could do those things with Kathy and Sabrina, though, because they always treated me the same no matter what.

Unfortunately, the same was not true of all my friends. Because I was immediately hospitalized after my diagnosis, most of my friends found out about my cancer through my mom. She called my friends' parents and explained what was going on. My diagnosis made some people feel awkward, and they didn't know what to say to me, even though I just wanted them to treat me the same way they had before the diagnosis. Some of the people I thought were my friends were making rude comments about my appearance behind my back. There was one guy who was afraid he could catch leukemia from me. A serious illness can really show you who your friends are.

My boyfriend had a very difficult time dealing with my leukemia. He and I had been together for a year before the news of my diagnosis. It was an awkward situation because I didn't feel comfortable talking to him about everything that was happening to me. On my fifteenth birthday, I had a party and everyone was kidding around, throwing cake icing at each other. My boyfriend was just about to put icing in my hair (he didn't know I wore a wig), and I had to stop him. I blurted out that it wasn't my real hair, and he stopped and just stared at me. Later, when we were alone, we talked about the fact that I hadn't told him; he was really upset. Eventually, we broke up. I think the stress was just too much for him, and I was devastated because we'd been together for so long.

There was a lot going on in my life, and while I could talk to my friends and family, I felt like I really needed to talk to other people my age who were going through the same things I was. Throughout my treatment, my parents tried to help me find a support group, but we didn't have much luck. I felt very isolated, and I wondered, "Isn't there anyone out there who survived this?" I had to discover other ways to deal with my feelings. Writing poetry has always been a good release for me, so I focused on letting my feelings out on paper.

▲▼▲▼▲▼▲▼

We got the results of Eric's bone marrow test on my fifteenth birthday. My mom brought home a birthday card she'd made on her computer at work. The front said, "An early birthday gift."

When I opened it up, I read, "Eric's a match!" Turns out, he matched in all five categories—a perfect donor. What a birthday present!

When it came time to do the transplant, my parents' insurance company told us that, for cost reasons, they wanted us to go to another hospital in the area instead of the University of Maryland, where I'd been going. No one in my family thought that it was a good idea to go to the other hospital; we were more comfortable where we were. I felt that the doctors and nurses I'd been seeing really cared about me, and I wanted them to perform the transplant.

We started a campaign to persuade our insurance company to let us stay at the University of Maryland Medical Center. We had everyone—my doctors and nurses, a hospital psychologist, family members, teachers, and friends—write letters to the insurance company practically begging to let me have the treatment at the Medical Center. Still, the insurance company refused. I was going to have to go to another hospital and be treated by people I didn't know.

Then something amazing happened. My doctors and the Medical Center agreed to perform the transplant for the same cost as the other hospital. I was able to stay and have the transplant with the doctors and staff I knew.

The transplant procedure began in November. Before they could extract Eric's bone marrow and inject it into me, my own cancerous marrow had to be destroyed. I had seven consecutive days of treatment (chemotherapy and radiation) right before the surgery. The actual transplant took place in December.

The doctors started with Eric, and he was unconscious through the whole procedure. They took a large needle and inserted it into one hip, then the other. They had to move the needle in and out of the bone to extract the marrow. Because Eric is a roller skater, his bones are very strong for someone his age, and the doctors had to push hard to get the needle in. When the doctors came out of surgery, they were exhausted.

I felt awful because the procedure was really painful for Eric. Although he was unconscious while it was actually going on, afterward he was sore for weeks, and he couldn't skate for months. Eric had a great attitude about the whole thing, but he said he'd never donate marrow again for anyone but me.

The doctors cleaned the bone marrow and brought it down to my room to inject me through an IV (intravenous) tube. I was surprised by how little marrow there was after it had been cleaned—it looked like about a pint. Eric was awake by that point and came down to my room to watch me be injected. He was so groggy from his procedure that he was really quiet, but he looked at the little bag of marrow and said, "All of that work for *that?*"

The whole thing was pretty anticlimactic. I was lying awake in bed, and the doctor just hooked up the bag to the IV and pumped the marrow into my body. I had spent all this time waiting to find a donor and getting all of that intensive treatment, and then the actual transfusion was done in a matter of minutes.

After that, we waited. My immune system was severely deteriorated because of the chemotherapy and radiation, so my white blood cell count was down to zero. If the transplant was successful, the count would start to rise within two weeks. At the end of the two weeks, my count was still low. We were worried that the transplant hadn't been successful. Finally, after three weeks, my count shot up and I started to recover.

It was depressing to be in the hospital over Christmas, but we made the best of things. Because my immune system was depleted, I was in a sterile room. Everything that was brought in had to be wiped clean with alcohol, and a large see-through wall and door separated me from other people. Only my immediate family members and the nurses were allowed on my side of the partition. Classmates, relatives, and friends of the family had all brought Christmas presents to the hospital, but I couldn't open them because of the germs. My dad stood outside the partition to open the presents and show me what I'd gotten. Fortunately, I was able to leave the hospital on New Year's Eve. I was glad that I didn't have to start the new year in the hospital.

I was at home for about four months after the transplant. My immune system was still depleted, and I had to avoid the germs you normally encounter just by being out and around a lot of people. I returned to school a little at a time, until I could be there full time without getting exhausted. In all, I missed about half of my freshman, all of my sophomore, and a lot of my junior years in high school. I managed to keep up with my schoolwork through the homebound program, where the school sends a teacher to your house to help you with tests and class work.

I've been doing really well since the transplant. You have to be symptom-free for five years before you're considered cured of the cancer. If all goes well, I'll officially be cured of leukemia December 7, 1999. But cancer is a tricky illness. Although it's difficult to say that you're ever absolutely cured, doctors consider the five-year mark a reasonable point to say that the cancer isn't very likely to recur. That would be a great way for me to start the millennium!

▲▼▲▼▲▼▲▼

I feel really fortunate to have been treated at the University of Maryland Medical Center. The whole staff there was great. I had two doctors, Dr. Frantz and Dr. Eskanazi. I can't speak highly enough of them. I always felt like I was an active member of my health-care team and that I had a say in my treatment.

The entire nursing staff was great, but especially one woman, Diane Keegan-Wells. She was always there for my family and me. If my treatment took a bad turn, she cried with us. I have a lot of respect for Diane. I saw her take care of patients day after day, without fail. I think she's one of the reasons that I want to go into pediatrics. It was inspiring for me to see a strong woman helping so many people.

I have a new boyfriend, Denis, who I've been with for about a year. We met when he was working as a counselor at a camp I attended for young people with cancer. His brother had leukemia, which is how Denis got involved with the camp. Denis knew why I was there—it was obvious because I was a camper—so there was no pressure for me to tell him about my leukemia. He's really a great guy; my family loves him and we're very happy together. We can talk about anything, even the really personal things that I don't feel comfortable discussing with anyone else.

I now work as a counselor at camps for children with cancer. I'm also on two lists—at the University of Maryland Medical Center and Johns Hopkins University—of people who volunteer to act as contacts for cancer patients and their families. My parents and I visit other cancer patients to discuss our experiences and offer support. It makes me feel good to know that I'm able to help other young people with cancer. You end up feeling so helpless when you have cancer, and for me, it's really empowering to help others who are going through an illness. This is one way I've been able to stay positive.

I'm also a spokesperson for the Children's Cancer Foundation. A few years ago, my parents and I attended a fund-raiser for the foundation because we thought that it would be a good opportunity to meet other families who are dealing with cancer. We were discouraged that they didn't have any patients speaking at the fund-raiser, which would have given a personal perspective to the issue of funding cancer research. We found the president of the foundation, Shirley Howard, and suggested having a patient talk about what it's like to have cancer. She basically said, "That's a great idea. How about you?"

That evening, both my mom and I spoke about our experiences to an audience of about 300 people. Our talks went over so well that we were asked to come back and speak at the next fund-raiser. Now I speak at two or three every year. It's great because I feel like I'm helping educate people about cancer.

One of the things I've learned from having leukemia is that life is too short not to try new things. You absolutely should live your life to the fullest. No matter what your medical difficulty might be, never give up. I'm sure that having a positive attitude has helped my recovery.

There will definitely be days when you feel like you're never going to make it and that you want to just quit. You can't. Do whatever you can to keep your spirits up. Things are going to get better—maybe not right away, but they will, as long as you hang in there.

R_x

Keep your head up and keep fighting. Today may be bad, but there will always be tomorrow.

—Kristy

Cancer Q & A

Q: What is cancer?

A: Cancer is a blanket term for a group of diseases characterized by the uncontrolled growth and spread of abnormal cells in the body. Every organ in the body is made up of cells, which normally divide to produce more cells only when the body needs them. A mass of tissue is formed when unneeded cells are created; this excess tissue is called a tumor. Not all tumors are cancerous (benign tumors aren't cancerous, but malignant tumors are). A biopsy is used to diagnose cancer. In a biopsy, the doctor removes a sample of tissue and examines it under a microscope to check for cancer cells. Leukemia is a kind of cancer that affects primarily the blood-forming tissues—bone marrow, lymph nodes, and spleen.

Q: What causes cancer?

A: Doctors think that leukemia and other cancers can be caused by both internal and external factors. Internal factors include hormones, immune conditions, and inherited mutations (changes in the body's genetic makeup). External factors include chemicals, radiation, and viruses. Several factors can work together to cause cancer.

Q: What are the effects of cancer?

A: Cells in malignant tumors can invade and damage healthy tissues and organs. These cells can also break away from the tumor and travel through the body to form new tumors elsewhere. When cancer spreads, it's referred to as metastasis. There are many symptoms common to those who have cancer (though they aren't always warning signs of cancer): change in bowel or bladder habits, a sore that doesn't heal, unusual bleeding or discharge, a thickening or lump in any part of the body, indigestion or difficulty swallowing, obvious change in a wart or mole, or a nagging cough or hoarseness.

Q: How many people have cancer?

A: Approximately 7.4 million Americans alive today have a history of cancer. More than 1 million new cases of cancer are diagnosed every year; approximately 8,800 of these cases are children. About 2,400 cases of leukemia are diagnosed in children every year.

Q: How is cancer treated?

A: Cancer is often treated by a combination of several methods. Surgery may be performed to remove areas of cancer, or patients may undergo radiation or chemotherapy, in which the body is exposed to chemicals in an attempt to slow or stop the progression of cancer. Immunotherapy, which is when the immune system is either stimulated or muted, may also be used. Hormones can be used to treat cancer, too. A bone marrow transplant is a form of treatment for some patients with leukemia.

Sources: American Cancer Society; Leukemia Society of America; National Cancer Institute.

Cancer Resources

Organizations

American Cancer Society
1599 Clifton Road, NE
Atlanta, GA 30329
1-800-ACS-2345 (Information line)
(404) 320-3333
http://www.cancer.org

This large organization has lots of information on the symptoms and treatments of all different sorts of cancer. The ACS publishes a variety of newsletters and magazines, organizes educational programs and events, and provides funds for research. The national office can put you in touch with the ACS chapter in your area.

Candlelighters Childhood Cancer Foundation
7910 Woodmont Avenue, Suite 460
Bethesda, MD 20814-3015
1-800-366-2223
(301) 657-8401
FAX: (301) 718-2686
http://www.candlelighters.org/

Founded by parents of children with cancer, this group offers support services for young people who have cancer (or who have survived cancer) and their families. The CCCF also maintains an information library and publishes newsletters, including *The CCCF Youth Newsletter*.

Leukemia Society of America
600 Third Avenue
New York, NY 10016
1-800-955-4LSA (Information line)
(212) 573-8484 (Main office)
FAX: (212) 856-9686
http://www.leukemia.org

Dedicated to education and patient support, the LSA offers free informational materials and answers questions about leukemia, Hodgkin's disease, lymphoma, and myeloma, plus offers referrals to treatment centers. The LSA sponsors educational seminars and support groups and can put you in touch with a group in your area.

National Cancer Institute/Cancer Information Service
1-800-4-CANCER
http://rex.nci.nih.gov

This government organization has many free printed materials on symptoms, diagnoses, treatments, and research. All calls are kept confidential, and callers receive personal attention from information specialists. The NCI's huge Web site has lots of information, including a special section on cancer and kids.

National Childhood Cancer Foundation
440 East Huntington Drive, Suite 300
P.O. Box 60012
Arcadia, CA 91066-6012
1-800-458-6223
(626) 447-1674
FAX: (626) 447-6359
http://www.nccf.org

This nonprofit organization, which seeks to educate the public about cancer and raise funds for research, provides free informational materials and publishes a newsletter. The NCCF Web site has lots of links to other organizations and resources, personal stories of kids who have survived cancer, and a "Meet Cancer Researchers" section where you can read about doctors and scientists who are trying to find a cure.

Book

Diagnosis Cancer: Your Guide Through the First Few Months by Wendy Schlessel Harpham, M.D. (NY: W. W. Norton and Co., Inc., 1997). Written by a doctor who is also a cancer survivor, this useful book includes definitions of common terms, information on tests and procedures (and their side effects), and thoughtful advice on the emotional issues involved with cancer diagnosis and treatment. The book is organized in a reader-friendly question-and-answer format and also includes a glossary and a list of resources.

Matthew
(Inflammatory
Bowel Disease)

Matthew Green is a seventeen-year-old high school junior. He has Crohn's disease, an inflammatory bowel disease. (Inflammatory bowel disease includes two chronic conditions—Crohn's disease and colitis, both of which affect the digestive system.) Matthew is an only child and enjoys surfing the Internet, playing the piano, collecting Star Trek memorabilia, and playing Nintendo. He plans to attend college to become a computer programmer. Matthew aspires to work in computer programming and, along the way, to change the world for the better.

The first time I got sick with Crohn's was during the summer of 1994. I had just finished seventh grade. My symptoms began with an upset stomach. At first, this was just a nuisance. I brushed it off as indigestion. A week later, I began to feel really tired. It got to the point where I didn't want to do anything; all I did was lie around and watch TV.

By mid-July, I was vomiting about once a week. That turned into twice a week, three times a week, then once a day, until it was happening after every meal. My usual doctor was out of town, so I had to see a new one. His diagnosis was that I had fallen into a pattern of "teenage bingeing and purging." I couldn't believe it—as if I would make myself throw up all the time!

A week or so later, I saw my regular doctor, who ordered some tests. By this time, school was back in session. On a clear August morning, I went to have an upper GI (a test where doctors use X-rays to see problems with your digestive system). It was my first experience with barium (yuck!), a really thick mixture that you drink to help infections or other problems in the digestive system show up on an X-ray. The results showed that I had an intestinal problem and was dehydrated. I was sent to the hospital, admitted immediately, and hooked up to an IV (intravenous) bag filled with a basic nutritional fluid to rehydrate me. I was so dehydrated that I drained the bag in less than forty-five minutes—a relatively healthy person would take about eight hours.

After I was out of danger of severe dehydration, my doctor turned my case over to my current gastroenterologist, a doctor who specializes in the digestive system. On September 1, 1994, at around 4 P.M., my "gastro" entered the room and revealed what was wrong with me—Crohn's disease. At the time, I was thirteen years old.

I had never heard of Crohn's. I was frightened about the diagnosis yet relieved that modern medicine had a name for my problem. My greatest fear had been that I was dying of some unknown disease.

I didn't know much about my illness, let alone how my life would change. I was scared to death that if my friends found out about my

Matthew at his bar mitzvah (a Jewish religious ceremony)

problem, I'd be alienated. Let's face it, in this day and age, with diseases such as AIDS, having a condition that can make you pale, thin, and weak tends to make people suspicious. I was too afraid to discuss my feelings about having Crohn's with anyone but my parents.

But I knew I couldn't live with the secret forever. One by one, I told my friends, explaining my illness and why I could no longer eat my favorite foods. I'm a quiet guy who doesn't cause trouble or say much in class, and I didn't tell everyone I knew about my diagnosis. The people I *did* tell at school didn't quite get what I was talking about. At the time, I didn't know a lot about Crohn's disease, so some of my explanations were pretty vague. I was asked a lot of questions, but for every answer I had, there were two more questions. I didn't know how to explain everything, but I handed out brochures from the Crohn's and Colitis Foundation of America, and that seemed to help people understand.

▲▼▲▼▲▼▲▼

For about two years after that, I was living a relatively normal life. Occasionally, I had a little pain, but overall things were going pretty well. I was taking a pill called Asacol, which keeps my digestive system from becoming inflamed, and I was following my diet—the same one I still follow today. I can't eat lactose, an acid usually found in dairy products; this means I can't have milk, cheese, butter, or anything made with those ingredients. I also can't have fried foods, vegetables, fruit (except for bananas), nuts, seeds, alcohol, chocolate, caffeine, coffee, Nutra Sweet, hot dogs, or fatty meats. Anything with a lot of sugar, and food that's blackened, barbecued, or pickled, is also off limits.

It may sound like I can't eat anything, but it's really not so bad. There are lots of foods that are Crohn's-friendly, such as specially made "lactose-free" products like ice cream and butter. My local health food store sells cheeses made from soybeans instead of milk, so I can still have certain kinds of pizza, soy cheeseburgers, and bagels with soy cream cheese. I really miss chocolate. I can have carob, which is a chocolate substitute, but it's not the same. I guess it's better than nothing, though.

One big problem I have is ordering food when I'm out with friends. If we're at my house, it's not a problem because I can talk my friends into ordering from a place that delivers foods I can eat. But when I'm out and about, I have to be able to adapt. If we're at a place where I absolutely can't eat anything, I just get a drink, sit back, and have a good time. I know I can always eat something when I get home. It may not be the perfect set of conditions, but I can live with this. Having to watch my diet is a lot better than being in the hospital for eating food that has made me sick.

My pain and diet were manageable, and my medication routines had become, well, routine. Then, in October of my sophomore year, I collapsed at school. I wasn't aware that this was one of the possible side effects of having Crohn's, and I was caught totally off guard. I hadn't missed a day of school since the beginning of the year, and now I suddenly had to go to the hospital and then spend time trying to recover at home.

No one knows what triggered my flare-up and collapse, although stress probably had something to do with it. I'd had auditions for the state choir that week, along with midterm exams. After the flare-up, I spent eleven days in the hospital, where I was on IV's of steroids and a glucose solution to keep me from getting dehydrated. I felt terrible and was depressed during my hospital stay. It was the most difficult time I've had so far with Crohn's. I tried to keep my spirits up with TV, Nintendo, and books. In the end, the best medicine was being able to go home.

▲▼▲▼▲▼▲▼

People with Crohn's disease don't all get the same symptoms when they have flare-ups. Typical symptoms include diarrhea, vomiting, and pain in the stomach or abdomen. Diarrhea and vomiting can lead to dehydration, and you can become seriously ill if you get really dehydrated because your body needs fluids to perform almost all of its normal functions.

When I left the hospital after my flare-up, I was taking 60 milligrams of Prednisone (a steroid) and one six-mercaptopurine (known as 6-MP) per day. Now I just take the 6-MP, which suppresses my immune system. With Crohn's, your immune system thinks that your body is sick, even though it isn't. What ends up happening is that your immune system starts to attack the healthy digestive tract, making your body sick in the process (6-MP helps fend off these attacks).

That flare-up took so much out of me that I didn't have enough energy to attend school. After I got out of the hospital, I spent three months recovering at home. At first, I tried getting school work from friends, but that wasn't always a reliable situation. Then I went on the homebound program (a teacher comes to the house to help you keep up in school).

This period was more difficult than my shorter absences had been. I was falling behind at that point, and the teacher was helping me out with algebra and science. It was frustrating for me to try to coordinate things with the school, and I wasn't happy with my semester grade in algebra (I eventually talked the school into letting me retake the class altogether). My German teacher was excellent, though. When she found out about my situation, she came over to help me right away, and we actually finished the semester before the rest of the class did. She'd spend about an hour or two with me every other day, and we accomplished a lot in a short time.

During my recovery, I used the Internet to distract me from my problems. I began searching for Crohn's information and found that it was all geared toward older patients. There was nothing out there for people my age. I decided to use my free time to create a Web site for teens who have Crohn's, and with three months on my hands, I definitely had the time to work on it.* My page debuted

*To visit Matthew's Web site, "Teens with Crohn's," go to *http://pages.prodigy.net/mattgreen*

on the World Wide Web on November 21, 1996, with three recipes for Crohn's-friendly foods, two links to other Web sites, and an editorial about liquid diets. In just one year, the site had almost 18,000 visitors and over 1,000 letters. I've since developed a new chat room and dozens of other features.

There's been a good reaction to the site. I've received mail from across the United States and also from Canada, Sweden, Colombia, Holland, England, Germany, Indonesia, Denmark, and other places. It's exciting, and I've made a lot of new friends. I like knowing that I'm helping people with their problems, whether it's offering them a new recipe or a chance to talk to someone who can understand what they're going through. The Web site has given me answers to my questions, and I'm more comfortable with my illness now. Connecting to other people through the World Wide Web has increased my self-esteem and boosted my self-confidence.

Because I know more about Crohn's than I did before, I'm much more comfortable talking with others about it. But, the truth is, I prefer to leave most people in the dark about my illness until it's really necessary to tell them. It can be tiring to answer the same questions all the time, explain my symptoms, and tell people why I've missed school.

Overall, my school has been very understanding about my situation. I have one special rule at school—I can go to the bathroom whenever I want, no questions asked. I usually miss only a few days of school here and there, and I just call my friends to get assignments during these short-term absences. My teachers are generally very understanding, and they try to make getting work and turning it in as easy as possible for me.

My grades haven't really changed; I still get A's and B's. I love a challenge, so I try to use stress to my advantage. Stress can energize you (unless it's really negative stress), and I try to turn negative stress into positive stress as much as possible. For example, when I feel stressed-out or anxious about my illness or a test that I didn't do so well on, I try to redirect my pent-up energy into something positive. I feel better if I work on my Web site or study hard for my next test.

It's really important to overcome your negative feelings, not just escape from them. When I'm feeling depressed, I talk to people about my illness, especially to people who have the same problems as I do. Sometimes I cope by doing something that just makes me feel happy (a little Nintendo can do the trick), but there's no real substitute for talking things out. Basically, I recommend that you talk to someone whenever you can—do whatever works to shift your focus from depression to happiness.

▲▼▲▼▲▼▲▼

My doctor is great. He always has an answer to my questions and knows what's new in the world of Crohn's research. He helps me deal with whatever problems I'm having. We got some free brochures from his office to give to the teachers at my school. Now, every year, my parents and I hand out a letter that we wrote, explaining some of the basics of Crohn's disease. We also hand out the Crohn's and Colitis Foundation of America brochure that's designed especially for teachers.

I wish that people with Crohn's could have just a few days off from our illness to enjoy all of our favorite foods again. I also wish that everyone could live for just a few weeks with Crohn's disease so they would understand how unbearable life sometimes feels for us. Obviously, neither of those things will happen, so I understand that the best way to deal with my illness is to accept it. I follow my diet and take my pills. I rest when I'm sick and try to be more active when I'm well. There isn't a magic potion that will make me feel better; it just takes time and a commitment to coping as best I can.

I try to keep in mind the advice I like to give others: Don't spend too much time feeling sorry for yourself. Having a chronic illness at an early age can give you a new outlook on life. You'll see that there's so much to do out there and, perhaps, so little time. If you can help someone else with a problem similar to your own, do so. Helping others is one of the reasons I started my Web site.

If you had asked me a year ago whether there were any positive aspects of having a chronic illness, I would have answered no. After all, how could a disease that causes digestion problems, bathroom difficulties, vomiting, weakness, and other nasty side effects be beneficial? But today, especially after last fall when my Web site went up, I can say, "Yes, there are positive aspects of having a chronic illness." Because of Crohn's, I've met dozens of people over the Internet. I even have a few close "net friends," and I talk to them daily.

I believe that young people who have a chronic illness mature faster. Because of the conditions life has dealt us, we're often forced to accept a set of rules for our diet, physical activities, and medication. Most people don't face these types of challenges until the end of their lifetime. Unlike most teens, we know that we're not invincible.

R$_\chi$

You can spend your life sitting at home complaining, or you can try to make a positive difference in the world. It's pretty cool knowing you're doing something that helps people.

—Matthew

Inflammatory Bowel Disease Q & A

Q: What is Inflammatory Bowel Disease?

A: Inflammatory Bowel Disease, or IBD, is a blanket term that covers both Crohn's disease and ulcerative colitis (UC). Crohn's disease can affect any part of the digestive system, from the mouth to the rectum. UC is a chronic disorder of the colon and rectum.

Q: What causes IBD?

A: The cause is unknown. Both Crohn's and UC are thought to be autoimmune disorders, which means that the immune system mistakenly thinks the body is sick and produces antibodies to fight illness. These antibodies end up attacking the body's healthy tissue. Crohn's and UC may also result from a genetic predisposition, which means that IBD patients may have been born with something that caused them to develop the illness. It's suspected that some kind of childhood virus triggers the development of IBD.

Q: What are the effects of IBD?

A: Crohn's disease and UC share many symptoms, including chronic diarrhea, fatigue, fever, weight loss, abdominal pain, dehydration, joint pain, and skin irritations. Both illnesses are characterized by spontaneous inflammation in various areas of the digestive system. Crohn's and UC can cause ulcers (holes) and inflammation in the digestive organs, but UC is generally only present in the lower part of the digestive system, while Crohn's tends to be more widespread.

Q: How many people have IBD?

A: Approximately 1 million people have IBD; 100,000 of these cases are children. The majority of people who have IBD are diagnosed between ages 10 and 18. An estimated 15,000 new cases are diagnosed each year.

Q: How is IBD treated?

A: There are many medications designed to relieve pain and calm symptoms; these medications may induce remissions, or periods during which the patient has no symptoms. IBD patients often have to follow restricted diets, avoiding common foods that tend to irritate the digestive system (such as dairy products, nuts, and high-fiber foods). In severe cases, surgery may be required to remove infected areas.

Sources: Crohn's and Colitis Foundation of America; *The Essential Guide to Chronic Illness* by James W. Long, M.D. (NY: HarperCollins, 1997).

Inflammatory Bowel Disease Resources

Organizations

Crohn's and Colitis Foundation of America
386 Park Avenue South, 17th Floor
New York, NY 10016-8804
1-800-932-2423
(212) 685-3440
FAX: (212) 779-4098
http://www.ccfa.org

The CCFA operates an information clearinghouse and publishes several brochures and newsletters. It also conducts education programs, sponsors support groups, and provides telephone counseling and doctor referrals. Take a look at the CCFA Web site for an online bookstore, information on local chapters, and tons of articles on all sorts of IBD-related topics.

United Ostomy Association, Inc.
19772 MacArthur Boulevard, Suite 200
Irvine, CA 92612-2405
1-800-826-0826
(949) 660-8624
FAX: (949) 660-9262
http://www.uoa.org

The UOA offers a free information packet and publishes a magazine *(Ostomy Quarterly)*, sponsors support groups, and operates a library of information about IBD. Call to find out about events and activities in your area or check out the Web site to read excerpts from the magazine, order other publications, or connect to other organizations and resources.

Books

The Angry Gut: Coping with Colitis and Crohn's Disease by W. Grant Thompson (NY: Plenum Press, 1993). This informative (and sometimes rather technical) book includes a chapter on the digestive system and how it functions, a history of the discovery and treatment of IBD, and information on symptoms, treatments, and insurance coverage. It also contains a glossary of IBD terms.

Crohn's Disease and Ulcerative Colitis: Everything You Need to Know by Fred Saibil, M.D. (Buffalo, NY: Firefly Books, 1997). This valuable book discusses the anatomy of the digestive system, medications, diet, and treatment options. Packed with helpful charts and diagrams, the book also includes a chapter on young people with IBD, a glossary of common IBD terms, and a list of resources.

Web site

Crohn's Disease Homepage
http://www.angelfire.com/ga/crohns

Maintained by a person with Crohn's, this Web site includes general information on the disease, advice from people with Crohn's disease, a list of people with Crohn's disease whom you can contact via email, and links to other IBD sites. Check out the Crohn's humor section.

Beryl

(Juvenile Rheumatoid Arthritis)

Beryl Hurwitch is a seventeen-year-old high school junior. She has juvenile rheumatoid arthritis (JRA), a condition in which afflicted joints become swollen, stiff, and painful to use. She lives with her younger sister, Sara, and her parents. Beryl enjoys singing, playing the piano, tennis, and acting. She plans to attend college but hasn't yet decided where to go or what to study.

I don't remember much about my diagnosis because I was only five years old. Sometimes my joints would hurt and get really stiff, so my mom brought me to the doctor. Dr. Lipnick, who's still my doctor today, asked me a lot of questions and started bending my arms and legs. When he bent my knee to my chest, it hurt so much that I screamed. Dr. Lipnick ran a blood test because he suspected that my problem was juvenile rheumatoid arthritis. Turns out he was right.

In first grade, the Arthritis Foundation picked me as the poster child for their telethon. A lot of people came to take pictures and to videotape me; a local news crew even talked to my class. Many people think that only elderly people get arthritis, so the news reporters did a story about what it was like for my classmates to know someone their age who has JRA. That year, I got to go to a conference sponsored by the National Arthritis Foundation in Nashville, Tennessee. I met a lot of new friends there and was even introduced to a few famous country singers. It was like I was famous for a while.

Third grade was difficult because I'd have to sit by myself and play what my teacher called "thinking games" while the other kids had physical education. When I got bored, my teacher let me use the time to help out with the kindergartners and read them stories. I liked that, but sometimes I just wanted to be in gym class with everyone else. I felt so different from the other kids, and it was hard knowing that all of them were better at running and other physical activities. Nobody made a big deal of it, though.

By the time I got to middle school and high school, kids wanted to know why some physical activities were harder for me. They didn't understand that my arthritis can cause a lot of pain in my joints and limit my movement. They'd say things like, "Why can't you just hit the ball?" Once in a while, I'd get upset and feel frustrated with myself for not being able to join in. But it doesn't make sense to be angry. I've learned to get over it and accept things the way they are. Now I have a deal with my physical education teacher: I'm allowed to sit out whenever I need to, no questions asked.

Sometimes I feel pretty good and am not really bothered by my arthritis, so I can do things like ride my bike and play tennis. Other times, I have flare-ups and my joints start to hurt and get stiff. The flare-ups don't follow a

Beryl

specific pattern, and I don't always know what brings them on (the weather, overactivity, etc.). I tend to have more problems when it's cold because my muscles contract, aggravating my arthritis. It's hard to say when I'm going to have a flare-up—I can be okay for days, or sometimes even weeks, but then suddenly start feeling worse.

▲▼▲▼▲▼▲▼

I've never really had a problem telling people about my arthritis. If they ask questions, I give them honest answers. Talking about my arthritis has helped me find out who my real friends are. They're friends with me because of who I am, not because of what I can or can't do physically.

This might sound funny, but having arthritis isn't always a bad thing. I've learned a lot from it. At last year's school science fair, for example, I decided to tie my project in with my arthritis and did a lot of research. I got together eight teens who have lower extremity JRA (which means that the lower part of their body is affected). I tested different types of heat on their knee joints to see which best reduces stiffness. I tried moist heat using a warm wet towel and dry heat using an electric heating pad. It turned out that everyone's arthritis was very different, with some types being more severe than others, so it was difficult to get accurate results. The research was a neat experience, though, and I felt like I was learning more about myself in the process.

My parents are really involved with the Arthritis Foundation, and they started a support group for parents of children who have arthritis. My mom and I go to yearly conferences sponsored by the foundation, and I've met a lot of young people with JRA this way. The conferences sponsor activity sessions so younger kids with arthritis can play together. As you get older, you can attend discussion groups and other activities. Because of the conferences, I have friends all over the country.

My friends who have JRA are able to understand how it feels, physically and emotionally, to be someone who's young and has arthritis. My regular friends are great, but if I have a problem because of my arthritis, they can't understand exactly how I feel. When I talk to my friends with JRA, I don't have to explain everything—they know what I mean. They understand what it's like to be in pain or to have trouble moving.

I've had arthritis for a long time, so I've gotten used to it—it's as much a part of me as my nose. I accept my limitations and have learned how to work around them. Accepting your limitations doesn't mean sitting around and doing nothing. You have to think about your strengths and make the most of them. I may not be able to play sports, but there are plenty of other things I *can* do.

I'm really involved with the school drama program. We do three productions a year—a comedy, a drama, and a musical. I also take voice lessons and sing soprano in the school choir. When I was in middle school, I was chosen to represent my school in the county and district choirs, which was a great honor for me. I'm going to audition this year, and I hope to be chosen again.

In high school, a lot of people think you're great if you can play sports. But there are so many other things you can excel at besides athletics. I've met a lot of people through music and drama. I like the activities that I participate in, and I don't feel like I'm missing out because I can't be a star athlete.

▲▼▲▼▲▼▲▼

My sister, Sara, who's nine, also has arthritis and was diagnosed at age two. It's pretty unusual for more than one child in a family to have arthritis. Doctors think that some aspects are hereditary, but arthritis doesn't just run in families—it's not that simple. You can inherit certain characteristics that might develop into arthritis, but doctors think that it takes something else, such as a certain virus you had as a kid, to actually cause those characteristics to develop into arthritis. I'm sure it was hard for my parents to learn that Sara has arthritis, too, but on the other hand, they already knew so much about it because of me that at least they were prepared for what was ahead for Sara. I think it may be easier for her to deal with her arthritis as she grows up because she knows that I have it and I'm okay. I'm an example for her.

To be honest, I've had arthritis for so long that I don't know how we'd be as a family if I *didn't* have arthritis. My mom and I take sort of a team approach to my treatment. We go to the doctor together, and she helps me remember any problems I've been having. At one point, I was taking a lot of pills for my arthritis. Between school and activities, it was hard for me to keep up with my pill schedule. My mom and I talked about it and, at my next appointment, we told the doctor about the problem. We all agreed that it would be easier for me to get a shot, even though that meant having to go to the doctor every other week. This option was a lot better than having to take all those pills every day.

I have a really good relationship with Dr. Lipnick. He has Crohn's disease, which affects his digestive system.* The fact that he has a chronic illness probably makes it easier for him to understand his patients and their needs. Dr. Lipnick knows that what most patients really want is for their doctors to care about them as people—not just see them as a set of symptoms. Sometimes he has his patients and their families over to his house for picnics. I think it's pretty rare for doctors to be so involved.

When I was fifteen, my mom and I cowrote an article for the American Juvenile Arthritis Organization's newsletter about the ten-year anniversary of my diagnosis. I described what the anniversary meant to me, and my mom explained what it meant to her. It was neat because we both learned a lot about what the other thinks and has gone through. You know what was surprising? I found out that she worries about my arthritis a lot more than I do! For me,

*For more on Crohn's disease, see pp. 72–83.

arthritis is just something I live with each day. If you think about it, *everyone* has something they have to deal with—my thing happens to be arthritis.

A chronic illness is hard to cope with when you're first diagnosed—I know that. But over time it gets easier, and before long it's even second nature. In some ways, I feel like I've matured faster than other people my age. I always have to consider my health—something that most kids take for granted. My arthritis might get a lot worse over the next few years; then again, it might not. I can't make predictions or stop these things from happening, but I *can* deal with them. Why worry about things that may never happen? I take things one day at a time.

R_X

You'd be surprised at how much a positive attitude can help you deal with your chronic illness.

—Beryl

Juvenile Rheumatoid Arthritis Q & A

Q: What is juvenile rheumatoid arthritis?

A: Rheumatoid arthritis is a condition in which the lining of the joints becomes inflamed—the affected joints feel warm and become tender, swollen, stiff, and painful to use. Juvenile rheumatoid arthritis (JRA) refers to this form of arthritis in juveniles (young people).

Q: What causes JRA?

A: The specific cause is unknown. Doctors believe that people may be born with characteristics that can develop into arthritis, but the triggers aren't well understood. It's possible that the combination of hereditary characteristics and exposure to a certain virus during childhood can cause arthritis. Some researchers think that diet can sometimes contribute to the development of arthritis, and some experts also believe that diet can change the way the immune system reacts in people with arthritis.

Q: What are the effects of JRA?

A: It can cause fatigue, low-grade fevers, loss of appetite and weight, and stiffness, pain, and swelling in the joints.

Q: How many people have JRA?

A: Approximately 2.1 million people have rheumatoid arthritis. An estimated 71,000 children in the U.S. have JRA.

Q: How is JRA treated?

A: There are many medications designed to relieve the pain and symptoms of juvenile rheumatoid arthritis. Physical therapy may be necessary due to the restricted movement arthritis often causes. In some cases, surgical procedures can remove damaged tissue from the joints. Many doctors feel that a balanced diet, combined with weight control, can help in the management of arthritis.

Sources: The Arthritis Foundation; Thomas J. A. Lehman, M.D., Cornell University Medical Center; *The Essential Guide to Chronic Illness* by James W. Long, M.D. (NY: HarperCollins, 1997).

Arthritis Resources

Organizations

American Juvenile Arthritis Organization
1330 West Peachtree Street
Atlanta, GA 30309
(404) 872-7100
FAX: (404) 872-0457
http://www.arthritis.org/ajao

Affiliated with the Arthritis Foundation, this group advocates in government, sponsors research, and conducts semi-annual conferences.
The AJAO provides educational materials and support for young
people with rheumatic diseases and their families. Call or write to
receive free information or to ask about AJAO's newsletter and other
publications.

The Arthritis Foundation
1330 West Peachtree Street
Atlanta, GA 30309
1-800-283-7800
(404) 872-7100
FAX: (404) 872-0457
http://www.arthritis.org

This organization sponsors research, advocates in government on
arthritis-related issues, educates the general public, and offers support
and information to people with arthritis. The Foundation provides free
materials and can refer you to the chapter in your area. Log on to the
Foundation's huge Web site for information about rheumatic diseases
and an online version of the Foundation's magazine *Arthritis Today.*

Book

250 Tips for Making Life with Arthritis Easier by Shelley Peterman Schwartz (Marietta, GA: Longstreet Press, Inc., 1997). This helpful book provides practical tips for coping with arthritis every day. Filled with useful information and ideas, it's particularly appropriate for young people who are preparing to live on their own.

Web sites

The Arthritis Society
http://www.arthritis.ca

This Canadian organization's Web site offers book and video reviews; information on diet, exercise, medications, and current research; and forums for the discussion of arthritis and arthritis-related issues.

Pediatric Rheumatology Home Page
http://www.goldscout.com

This no-frills site is sponsored by Thomas J. Lehman, M.D., a physician who specializes in rheumatic diseases. The site provides information on rheumatic illnesses, including arthritis and lupus, and also provides links to other sites for rheumatic illness.

Seth
(Congenital Heart Defect)

Fifteen-year-old Seth Barmash is in tenth grade. He has tetralogy of Fallot, a congenital heart defect (CHD). Seth plays drums and guitar and is currently forming a band. He enjoys Frisbee, roller hockey, roller blading, and BMX-style bike riding. Because he likes working on the computer, Seth operates a Web page for teens with CHD. He plans to finish high school and go on to college, but he hasn't yet decided on a career (perhaps something in the music industry). Seth lives with his mom and dad, his younger sister, Jessica, and an older cousin, Shara.

My birth was traumatic. Around the day I was due to be born, I was delivered by emergency cesarean section because I'd gotten an infection. The doctors told my parents that I was dying, and there was nothing they could do. The first time my parents saw me, my skin was blue and I was in a coma. My mom remembers telling me how much she loves me, because she didn't want me to die without hearing that.

About an hour or two later, the doctor reported that I had started to get better because of the antibiotics I was given, but he thought that I might have heart problems. My parents gave him permission to run some tests, which showed that I had multiple heart defects. Fourteen hours after I was born, I was diagnosed with a congenital heart defect called tetralogy of Fallot (TOF). TOF is a term for four separate heart defects. Because my heart wasn't working right, it couldn't pump enough blood to my lungs, so my blood didn't have as much oxygen in it as it should. That's why my skin looked blue.

Three of the four defects have been repaired through three separate surgeries. I had my first heart operation when I was four days old; it was a shunt (surgical passage), which increased the amount of blood flow to my lungs by making a connection between my aorta and pulmonary artery. The aorta is the large artery that sends blood to the rest of the body, and the pulmonary artery sends blood to the lungs. My parents didn't get to hold me until I was six days old. I spent a total of eight days in the intensive care unit before the doctors moved me to a regular floor.

My second surgery was in 1985, when I was three. That operation repaired a hole between my left and right ventricles, the two lower chambers in the heart. With the hole, the blood was flowing back and forth between the two (normally, the two chambers are separate, and the blood can't flow between them). In addition, the surgeon placed a conduit (tube) into my pulmonary outflow tract, which was too small to allow enough blood to flow into my lungs. My third surgery, when I was eleven, was to make my pulmonary artery and conduit bigger to help increase

Seth

the amount of blood flowing to my lungs. I'll need more surgery in the future, but we're not sure when.

I don't remember much about my first two surgeries because I was so young. But I do have memories of my hospitals stays—some good and some bad. There was the time when I was recovering from my last surgery, and the surgeon didn't want me to have any medicine for my pain; my parents had to insist and put up quite a fight before I got the painkillers I needed. That was a really horrible experience. But not every hospital visit has been so bad. Once, when I was in for a procedure, I had my CD player and my favorite stuffed animal to keep me occupied. When I forgot to bring them with me to the lab for tests, one of the nurses was nice enough to run back to my hospital room and get the CD player and stuffed animal for me. I have really good memories of that hospital stay because everyone took such good care of me. I know that each hospital visit is a step forward in treating my CHD, so I accept that it's all just part of my treatment.

▲▼▲▼▲▼▲▼

My congenital heart defect has affected my life in different ways. Mostly, having CHD has limited my ability to participate in sports and other strenuous activities; for me, that's the hardest thing to deal with. Sports that involve a lot of running, like soccer and lacrosse, are hard for me. To make up for this, I've gotten into activities like roller hockey and Frisbee, where the running is minimal. But on a really hot day, I can't do anything—my body gets so fatigued that I can't even leave my home. I put up with these things, and I manage to work around them, but it isn't easy.

Participating in after-school sports activities is mandatory at my school. One time, we had to attend weeklong tryouts for a sport during spring term, and I chose baseball because I'd played Little League for many years. Baseball is one of the sports that I'm allowed to play, though I have CHD. I worked really hard during the tryouts and showed up each day, only to find out that I didn't make the team. I was upset because some of the guys who made the team hadn't attended all of the tryouts and—in my mind—didn't play baseball as well as I did. I think the coach didn't want me to play because he thought that something might happen to me because of my CHD. I felt discriminated against and was angry that the school required sports participation but then cut some people from the teams. I wondered why I'd worked so hard for nothing.

My CHD affects my life at school in other ways, too. Extracurricular activities are hard because, after a long day of classes, my body is worn out. Common illnesses like the flu or a cold usually mean a day out of school for other kids, but for me, an illness can mean being absent for two or three days, maybe more. In ninth grade, the public school I went to began "intensive scheduling," where each class was twice as long (eighty-five minutes). With the new schedule, if I missed three days of school, it was almost like missing six days' worth of classes. I was afraid that I'd end up falling behind because I usually miss an average of six to eleven days per term (which would be like missing twelve to twenty-two days with the new schedule). Plus the intensive scheduling meant that I'd probably be too tired from extended classes to even attempt homework. After we thought about how the new schedule would affect me, my parents and I began to look at private schools. We found one we liked, and I switched schools. It's worked out pretty well.

Sometimes I think my teachers don't understand that my CHD can affect my grades. I have trouble studying for tests and keeping up with homework when I'm really fatigued. My mom usually talks to my teachers at the beginning of the school year, explaining TOF and how it affects me. That way, they can get a better understanding of my situation and needs.

My friends are very supportive, and they understand my problems. Because I've grown up with the same friends all my life, they've learned to deal with my CHD over the years. I'm pretty open with people about things, and I don't have a hard time talking about my CHD. If I meet someone new, and the person sees the scars from my surgeries, I just explain that I have TOF and that surgery has corrected some of the problems with my heart. I don't make a big deal out of it.

I take a medication called Vasotec to help my heart work more efficiently. A side effect of the medication is that it makes my cheeks look permanently red, like I'm blushing. It's not that big of a problem—just an annoyance.

Because I was born with CHD, I don't know what life would be like without it. Sometimes I wish that I could take part in the activities that my friends participate in, but overall, I'm pretty comfortable with who I am and what I can do. I don't think of my CHD as a handicap or that my life is awful because of it. I do the only thing I can, which is find ways to work around it. That's the way life goes.

▲▼▲▼▲▼▲▼

I don't know any kids with CHD, so I thought that creating a Web page would be a great opportunity for me to talk to other kids like me.* My page has been up and running since November 1996, and it's growing each day. I've met a few people through the World Wide Web, and I'm excited about that. It helps to know that there are people out there like me. Everything I've gone through they've gone through, too.

As bad as things sometimes are for me, I know that my problems could be a lot worse. I can still live a basically normal life because I've learned to adapt. There will always be things about me that are a little different from others, but I won't let that change the quality of my life.

---

*To visit Seth's Web page, go to *http://www.tchin.org/teen.htm* (it's part of the "teen lounge" section of the Children's Health Information Network site).

R~x~

**You have to work with what you have
and be thankful for it. You are who
you are.**

—Seth

Congenital Heart Defects Q & A

Q: What are congenital heart defects?

A: Congenital heart defects exist at birth and occur when the heart or blood vessels don't develop normally before a baby is born.

Q: What causes congenital heart defects?

A: Often, doctors don't know what causes congenital heart defects. In some cases, though, an unborn child catches a virus, such as German measles, which interferes with the development of the baby's heart. In some cases, poor nutrition during pregnancy can cause congenital heart defects.

Q: What are the effects of congenital heart defects?

A: There are at least thirty-five types of congenital heart defects. Most of these either partially obstruct the flow of blood in the heart or in the vessels near the heart, or cause the blood to flow through the heart in a way that's not normal. When the heart doesn't work properly, fluid can build up in the lungs, making it hard to breathe. Fluid can then build up in the rest of the body and cause swelling.

Q: How many people have congenital heart defects?

A: Approximately 32,000 babies are born every year with congenital heart defects. It's estimated that 960,000 Americans have congenital heart defects.

Q: How are congenital heart defects treated?

A: Congenital heart defects are often treated with drugs, such as diuretics and digoxin. A diuretic is a medication that causes the body to excrete water and salt by causing an increase in the rate at which urine is produced; this helps the body get rid of excess fluid. Digoxin causes the heart muscle to contract with more force, helping it pump blood; the medication also slows the rate of heartbeats and helps remove excess fluid from tissues. Some people with congenital heart defects may need open heart surgery to correct the malformed areas of the heart.

Source: American Heart Association.

Congenital Heart Defects Resources

Organizations

American Heart Association
7272 Greenville Avenue
Dallas, TX 75231
1-800-AHA-USA1 (Calls will be automatically routed to your local
chapter or to the Heart and Stroke Information Center)
http://www.amhrt.org
http://americanheart.org/Health/Lifestyle/Youth/index.html (Youth section
of the AHA Web site)

The AHA sponsors research, advocates on behalf of the public for heart
disease issues, and educates both professionals and the general public.
The Association offers free informational materials for and about
young people with heart disease, as well as some items for sale. Check
out the AHA's enormous Web site, where you can find the latest news
and research information.

Children's Health Information Network
1561 Clark Drive
Yardley, PA 19067
(215) 493-3068
http://www.tchin.org

CHIN produces Congenital Heart Disease Information and Resources,
a Web site that provides interactive forums, resources, links to other
sites, and peer-reviewed informational materials for families and
adults with CHD.

**Kids With Heart National Association for
Children's Heart Disorders**
1578 Careful Drive
Green Bay, WI 54304
1-800-538-5390
(920) 498-0058
http://www.execpc.com/~kdswhrt/kwhhome

This organization provides parent-to-parent matching services that allow families to contact other families (via mail, phone, or email) who are also dealing with CHD. The Kids With Heart newsletter contains articles by medical experts and parents. Check out the Web site, which features the newsletter and links to other CHD-related sites.

Book

The Heart of a Child: What Families Need to Know About Heart Disorders in Children by Catherine Neill (Baltimore, MD: Johns Hopkins University, 1993). This book provides general information on congenital heart defects and developments in the treatment of heart problems in children. It also includes examples of actual cases and offers hope to kids with heart defects and their families.

Stacy and Wendy
(Lupus)

Stacy Adesso is twenty-seven years old and Wendy Lee is twenty-four. They've been friends for eleven years and both have lupus, an inflammatory disease that can affect every system and organ in the body. Stacy graduated from Shepherd College with a bachelor's degree in parks, recreation, and leisure services with a concentration in therapeutic recreation. She works for Loudoun County Parks and Recreation and Community Services, where she plans and implements community recreation programs for special needs populations. Stacy enjoys being outdoors and spending time with her family and friends. She has one sister, Aimee.

Wendy recently graduated with a master's degree in public health. She is about to enter medical school with the goal of becoming a doctor. A musician who plays piano, violin, and guitar, Wendy also enjoys ice-skating, reading, and working out. She has a sister named Diane.

STACY: I lived with a serious but undiagnosed illness for the first thirteen years of my life. I experienced symptoms that included joint pain, fevers, and, as I got older, respiratory problems. Unfortunately, my doctors looked at each symptom individually. It never occurred to them that my ailments were related; the doctors even told me that the joint pains were just "growing pains." Over the years, my mom kept a journal of all of my symptoms and researched them as they came up. On her own, she developed a suspicion that I had a rheumatic illness because of the pain and inflammation I experienced in various places throughout my body.

When I was growing up, my mom worked for the Foreign Service in the U.S. State Department, so we traveled a lot. We were living in Brazil when I was in seventh and eighth grade. I was sick often, and my mother became more determined than ever to get good medical attention for me. We had plans to go to Disney World, and my mom located a hospital in Florida that was supposed to have a good department of rheumatology. She made an appointment to see one of the doctors there, so in that trip we killed two birds with one stone, so to speak—we got a vacation and doctor visit. The doctor told me that I had a form of arthritis and instructed us to treat it with aspirin.

After I returned to Brazil, I began to have problems with my breathing. The doctors there discovered that I had fluid in my lungs. I had to be treated in Brazil because I couldn't fly home with fluid in my lungs—the change in air pressure could have been dangerous. What an experience! You see, the hospitals in Brazil aren't as good as the ones in the United States. The operating room didn't have any doors, so I was sitting there for four hours with a drainage tube coming out my back, and the doctors wheeled in a woman who was about to give birth (she was moaning with labor pains). It was awful.

My mom wanted to arrange for a transfer back to the U.S., and two days after my experience in the Brazilian hospital, we flew to Washington, D.C. The government agreed that I'd receive better medical care

Stacy (left) and Wendy

back in the States, so they arranged a transfer for my mom. My younger sister, Aimee, and I stayed with my aunt in New Jersey while my mom tied things up in Brazil and looked for a house in the States. We ended up settling in suburban Virginia, near Children's Hospital. I started ninth grade not knowing anyone. I was unfamiliar with American slang because of my years overseas, and I felt so frustrated about feeling sick all the time.

At Children's Hospital, I met Dr. White, my rheumatologist. She treats pain in the muscles and joints, and she was the first doctor to realize that I have lupus. Aside from the kind of lupus caused by medication, there are two basic kinds. Mild lupus is usually characterized by skin rashes and sensitivity to the sun. Its more menacing form, called systemic lupus erythematosus, can affect any part of the body, including the lungs, heart, and kidneys. Lupus makes you have a hyperactive immune system; it's like your body attacks itself.

I have the more serious form of lupus. I've had problems with rheumatoid arthritis,* butterfly rashes on my face, sun sensitivity, and respiratory problems. Since my diagnosis, I've been taking Prednisone, a powerful steroid that can cause a lot of nasty side effects. I've experienced several of them—a rounded and puffy face, hair loss, weight gain, and mood swings.

Dr. White had another lupus patient, Wendy, and she introduced the two of us one day when we were both in the waiting room. Wendy and I have been friends ever since, and it's helped me to be around someone who knows exactly what it's like to have lupus. Wendy and I are like day and night when it comes to dealing with our illnesses. She reads everything she can about lupus and is always telling me new information. I, on the other hand, denied my diagnosis from the start. I thought, "I'm not going to take responsibility for my health. I'm not sick. I don't have to listen to what the doctors are telling me."

---

*For more on arthritis, see pp. 84–93.

My mom took charge of my medical care. She arranged the doctor appointments, took notes, and asked all the questions. I did the minimum—took my medication, showed up for appointments, and had blood tests. Because Children's Hospital is a teaching hospital, where people studying to be doctors learn from real patients, several teams of medical students would come in and ask all sorts of questions. My mom would pull out the notes about my medical history that she'd been keeping ever since I was a baby—when I started feeling sick, my symptoms, doctors I'd seen, medical tests, and medications I'd taken. All of this information was organized in a binder; as different teams came to see me, we'd just hand it over, which saved a lot of time. The medical students were impressed with how organized the binder was. Because of the notes, all the patterns of my lupus were clear.

▲▼▲▼▲▼▲▼

During my first year of high school, I was sick a lot. I didn't want people at school to know about my lupus. When my arthritis caused inflammation in my hands, I would wear splints. I used to tell my classmates that I had a volleyball injury because adolescents can be cruel when you're different. I thought a sports injury sounded cooler than a chronic illness, and the other students seemed to believe my explanation of how I'd "hurt myself."

I was definitely unhappy. My illness seemed to hinder everything I did, and it was hard for me to adjust to public school. (From first through eighth grades, I'd attended a private school for the children of American diplomats overseas.) I tried desperately to fit into the public school atmosphere. As a result, I made a lot of choices that had a negative impact on my health. In social situations, I found it difficult to say no—I'd go to the beach and bake in the sun, stay up late, take on too many activities at once, and not tell my friends and teachers about my illness.

Only when I had a flare-up would I tell people what was really going on with me. Then, when I explained it, I'd sugarcoat the symptoms and effects to make it sound like my illness wasn't that serious. I didn't want people to be afraid of me—I couldn't face the possibility of rejection.

The poor choices I made resulted in more flare-ups, and even hospitalizations. At the time, I was put on a variety of medications and was given a number of tests to determine the cause of the flare-ups. I had regular checkups consisting of blood tests, urine analyses, field vision, and bone-density tests.

My bad habits continued while I was away at college. This time, though, I didn't have my mom there to make me wear sunblock, long sleeves, and a hat in the sun. She wasn't there to try to keep me from overdoing my activities in general. With college came independence, alcohol, parties, and a whole new set of rules for fitting in. Once again, I failed to tell my friends—even my roommates—about my illness. And, once again, it took a flare-up for me to let them find out the truth.

I had two major flare-ups in college. One was in 1991, when the lupus attacked the blood vessels in my hands. This limited the blood flow to my fingers and, as a result, they turned white, then purple. Then they began to blister, which was very painful; the blisters would dry up and flake off.

This process, known as Raynaud's phenomenon, can happen to me whenever my hands get cold. It doesn't even have to be winter for my hands to start showing signs of Raynaud's. I need to be careful if I put my hands in a freezer or near an air conditioner. When the symptoms get really bad, I take a blood pressure medication to thin out my blood and help my circulation.

My second flare-up occurred one evening in December of 1992. I was walking back to my college apartment after dinner, and my left foot went numb. I thought it had fallen asleep, but the feeling didn't go away. Later that night, I woke up screaming from pain. My roommates were surprised and didn't know what to do. They called my mom and the college nurse, who gave me a strong painkiller. My mom made an appointment for me to see a rheumatologist and a neurologist, who looks for any irregularities in the brain.

The next night, it happened again. My mom came and got me and took me straight to George Washington University Hospital in Washington, D.C. I was hospitalized immediately, and the doctors thought I might be permanently paralyzed. They ran tests to see what was wrong with me. As time passed, my symptoms worsened—I was unable to move from the waist down. It felt as if my legs, from the knees down, were permanently asleep. I was on extremely high doses of Prednisone, and my doctors decided that I should undergo chemotherapy.* At that point, I didn't care what they did—I just wanted to get better. I had seven chemotherapy treatments and, during that time, I definitely learned to have respect for cancer patients. It was an extremely unpleasant experience, but it helped me get better. It turned out that I had developed what's called mononeurititis multiplex, which is partial paralysis of the legs and feet.

I didn't go back to the same college after the second flare-up. Instead, I finished my classes closer to home at Northern Virginia Community College (NOVA), which had a program that allowed me to take classes at NOVA and then transfer the credits I earned back to my former school.

For a year and a half, I had regular appointments with a physical therapist to counteract the damage to my legs. The hardest thing was not being able to drive; I had to rely on others for transportation. Also, I'd lost most of my hair as a side effect of the chemotherapy, which made me feel self-conscious. For a while, I was confined to a wheelchair, and I had to wear splints to support my ankles. I came to realize how inaccessible many facilities are for the physically challenged. Without the encouragement of my mom, I would have sat at home, feeling depressed. She encouraged

*For more on chemotherapy, see pp. 55–71.

me to fight my illness every step of the way—finish college, buy a wig, be in my friend's wedding . . . participate.

During my last few chemotherapy sessions, I had to make a big decision. My mom was offered an assignment overseas, and this meant that if I stayed behind, I'd be alone and would have to take full responsibility for my health care. She went, and I did just that—I took responsibility for myself, and it turned out to be the best thing for me. Eventually, I was walking again, and then I was able to run and drive. My hair grew back, too.

In the fall of my senior year, I visited my old college for homecoming, and seeing my old classmates was really hard. They didn't even ask me where I'd been, and they hadn't sent me cards or called me while I was gone. I was hurt, and I realized that these people weren't true friends. I finished my classes at NOVA in December of 1993, and I returned to my old college again the next spring for my graduation ceremony.

▲▼▲▼▲▼▲▼

Sometimes I still find it difficult to make friends and fit in. Now and then, I've been disappointed by people who just don't want to be bothered with someone who isn't healthy. Same goes for relationships with guys. It's hard for me to find friendships and relationships that are genuine. My mom and sister have always been there for me, though. Many times, they even put aside their own needs to pay attention to mine, and I regret that I so often took them for granted.

One thing that has really helped me is getting involved in a support group. Support groups are a great way to get to know people who've had similar experiences and feelings. Because these people are dealing with illnesses too, they know what it's like to try to look just fine on the outside when inside there's a war going on. Wendy and I attend support groups together sometimes.

I envy Wendy because she's always really open about her lupus and tells people almost immediately. I like to get to know people

first, and I'll tell them about my lupus only if it comes up naturally. I'm trying more and more to take the risk of telling others
about my illness, whether it's friends or boyfriends. It's still
stressful, but I've been surprised to learn that many people I meet
know someone else who has lupus. For instance, my college sociology teacher has lupus, which is why she always kept the lights off
in the classroom (because of a sensitivity to the ultraviolet bulbs).
At my first job after college, I found out that a coworker's daughter
has lupus.

I've learned how to live well with a disruptive, unpredictable
illness. I try to listen to my body and to better understand my
physical and emotional needs. I'm now able to say no to things that
aren't good for me. Some people who have lupus go into remission,
a period where they have no symptoms for months or years. Maybe
I'll go into remission, or maybe I won't. The best I can do is live
for today and plan for tomorrow.

It's been thirteen years since my diagnosis, and there's still no
cure for lupus. I think everyone on earth, at some point, has to deal
with something tough or that puts limitations on them. That's the
way life is, and not just for people with chronic illnesses.
Limitations, choices, decisions, successes . . . they affect us all.

Don't dwell on what life would be like if you didn't have a
chronic illness or what it was like before you were diagnosed. I've
closed the door on my old life—that's no longer who I am, and
there's nothing wrong with that. I try hard to find a balance—of
family, friends, relationships, my career, my goals, my future—and
to let my illness simply be a natural part of my daily routine.

WENDY: Meeting my friend Stacy was one of the best things
to happen to me after I found out that I have lupus. My
diagnosis had left me feeling so alone. I didn't know
anyone else with lupus, and I had no idea what was going to
happen to me. Stacy and I hit it off immediately, and so did our
mothers. Since then, I've met many other young people with lupus,

but I think it was really important that I met Stacy so soon after my diagnosis.

I was diagnosed when I was twelve. I was in eighth grade and involved in everything—honors classes, the school newspaper, track, and soccer. My focus was on making friends and being successful. The last thing on my mind was a chronic illness, and at the time, I didn't even know what lupus was (neither did my friends and family). Lupus seemed like an inconvenience, like wearing glasses can be. I never imagined that my chronic illness would change the entire course of my life.

▲▼▲▼▲▼▲▼

It all started one morning when I woke up with pain in my toes. I blamed it on cross-country racing and waited for the pain to go away. It didn't. Instead, the pain spread to other joints in my body and became worse each day.

I started to get fevers, and every night they got higher—99 degrees, 100, 103. My parents were very concerned and wanted to take me to the doctor, but I kept insisting that I was okay and would be fine the next day. Finally, one morning, I just couldn't get out of bed because I was so tired and in so much pain. My parents decided that it was time for me to see the doctor, whether I wanted to or not.

The strange thing was, the symptoms seemed to come and go. By the time the doctor saw me, I was actually feeling a bit better. My parents and I described the pain and fatigue that I'd been having, but the doctor couldn't find anything obviously wrong with me. He even accused us of being hypochondriacs, imagining everything. He sent me home without any tests or medication.

That evening, my temperature rose to 105 degrees, and I was screaming from pain in my abdomen. My parents rushed me back to the clinic, where the same doctor was on duty. He saw for himself that I had a fever and that my joints were swollen. He suspected that I had some sort of connective tissue disease but couldn't make a definite diagnosis. Instead, he referred me to a rheumatologist— Dr. White.

Dr. White was wonderful, especially compared to the doctor I'd just seen. I felt slightly uncomfortable in the waiting room, where all of the other patients seemed to be at least fifty years older than me. In retrospect, it's kind of funny because everyone thought that my mother was the patient instead of me. Dr. White listened to my history, recognized the seriousness of my illness, and immediately had me hospitalized for tests. After three weeks, I was diagnosed with systemic lupus erythematosus. Even worse, the lupus had affected my kidneys, so I had to return to the hospital for a kidney biopsy, during which they stuck a needle in my back to remove a piece of my kidney.

I've heard people say that it's common to go through a period of denial or disbelief after being diagnosed, but I don't think I went through that phase. If I did, it was a different type of denial—I accepted that I had lupus, but I refused to accept that there was nothing I could do about it.

After my diagnosis, it was really hard for me to go back to school. I'd fallen behind in my classes, and while I'd always been a straight-A student before, I now found myself struggling just to keep up. Although some of my teachers were kind and made accommodations for my illness, others were unreasonable. My honors math teacher wouldn't take time to help me catch up and told me to drop the class. My physical education teacher forced me to run the mile with the other healthy students, timed me, and based my grade on my time.

It drove me crazy that my friends and classmates were treating me differently. While I was in the hospital, I didn't have time to call them to let them know what was going on, and when one of my friends phoned my house to find out where I was, she misunderstood what my parents told her. My friend then went back to school and told everyone that I had leukemia* (a form of cancer) and was going to die. When I returned, I had to explain over and over again that I actually had lupus.

Having lupus was bad enough, but dealing with everyone else was infinitely worse. The fact that my appearance had changed didn't help matters. Because I was on steroid medication, my face and body were puffy, and it was very obvious that something was wrong with me. I thought that I looked like a "Pillsbury dough girl." My self-esteem and confidence were completely gone. Inside I was the same person, but everyone started treating me like I was less than a person because of my appearance.

In the process, I found out who my true friends were. Some of the people I knew stopped calling and avoided me. Other friends weren't allowed to play with me because their parents were afraid I was contagious. My friends who stayed and supported me through that difficult period are still my closest friends. It was tough not being accepted by some of my peers and not being part of the "in" crowd. Eventually, I learned to stop caring about what other people thought of me, and I focused more on what kind of person I was.

▲▼▲▼▲▼▲▼

Sometimes I think that my family suffered even more than I did. They had to watch what my illness was doing to me and how I was coping with it. I hated it when my mom would drive me to school and walk me into the building, holding an umbrella over me to protect me from the sun. My classmates would stare, and I knew that they thought I was a freak; they didn't understand my sensitivity to sunlight. At the time, I thought that my family was being overprotective and not letting me be like everyone else. I became very rebellious and did things I wasn't supposed to, just to prove that I could.

*For more on leukemia, see pp. 55–71.

I was determined to live a "normal" life, even though I had lupus. I went to the beach and didn't take my medication. As a result, I got sick a lot and spent time in the hospital. When I look back on it now, I'm sorry about what I did. I now know that I put my parents through a lot by doing such things to myself.

I'm an adult now, but there are still issues that I have to deal with because of my lupus. Despite everything I've gone through and all the things that people have told me I can't do, I'm alive, doing well, and even beating the odds. Sometimes I wonder, "Why is this happening? I don't think I did anything wrong, so why am I being punished?" But I know in my heart that I'm not being "punished" and that there's a reason for everything. Having a chronic illness isn't easy, but then again, nothing in life is. Suffering makes you appreciate all of the good things that life has to offer.

I've known since my diagnosis that I want to make sure that no one else has to go through what I've been through, physically and mentally. I hope to increase public awareness of lupus, become a better, more sensitive doctor than some of the ones I've had, and eventually find a cure. To reach my goal, I've studied a lot of medical literature on my own and have gotten involved in activities sponsored by the Lupus Foundation of America. As I've grown older, I've also conducted laboratory research, and now I'm getting ready to go to medical school.

There's no cure for lupus, and for now, it's an illness I'll have to live with. But I know that having lupus has made me a better and stronger person. I've learned to appreciate life, which has helped to shape my ambitions. I wouldn't be the person I am today if I didn't have lupus.

R_x

When it comes to having a serious illness, you can't leave it behind or pretend it's not there; you don't have a choice about it. But you can choose to make the best of your situation and to take good care of yourself.

—Stacy

Above all, don't give up your dreams. You may have to take some time off here and there, adjust your goals a little, or change the way you're going to achieve them, but don't think you can't realize your dreams just because of your illness. You can.

—Wendy

Lupus Q & A

Q: What is lupus?

A: Lupus is a disease that causes inflammation in various parts of the body. The name comes from the Latin word for "wolf," because of the severity with which lupus attacks the body.

Q: What causes lupus?

A: The exact cause is unknown. However, lupus is classified as an autoimmune disorder, which means that the immune system mistakenly thinks the body is sick and produces antibodies to fight illness. These antibodies end up attacking the body's healthy tissue. Lupus may also result from a genetic predisposition, which means that the lupus patient may have been born with something that encourages the development of the illness.

Q: What are the effects of lupus?

A: There are three kinds of lupus. Discoid lupus, a milder form, affects only the skin. Systemic lupus erythematosus can affect almost every system and organ in the body, including the joints, kidneys, brain, heart, blood vessels, skin, and lungs. Drug-induced lupus can be caused by certain medications but is extremely rare (symptoms tend to disappear once the patient stops taking the medication). Lupus can cause distinctive skin problems such as the "butterfly rash," which forms a butterfly pattern as it spreads across the nose and cheeks. The disease can also produce fatigue, fever, loss of appetite, pain and swelling in the joints, and bruising.

Q: How many people have lupus?

A: According to the Lupus Foundation of America, more people have lupus than AIDS, cerebral palsy, multiple sclerosis, sickle-cell anemia, and cystic fibrosis combined. There are between 1.4 and 2 million diagnosed cases, and the illness occurs ten to fifteen times more often in women than men. Approximately 16,000 new cases are diagnosed each year.

Q: How is lupus treated?

A: There are many medications designed to induce remissions, or periods during which the patient has no symptoms. Lupus patients are often instructed to follow special diets, restricting the amount of salt and fat they eat. Physical therapy may be necessary to combat symptoms that affect movement, such as joint problems.

Sources: Lupus Foundation of America; *The Essential Guide to Chronic Illness* by James W. Long, M.D. (NY: HarperCollins, 1997).

Organization

Lupus Foundation of America
1300 Piccard Drive, Suite 200
Rockville, MD 20850
1-800-558-0121 (Information line)
(301) 670-9292
FAX: (301) 670-9486
http://www.lupus.org

The Lupus Foundation of America has free informational brochures and lots of books and other resources for sale. The LFA also publishes a newsletter *(Lupus News),* sponsors support groups, and provides lists of physicians through its chapters nationwide.

Books

Coping with Lupus: A Guide to Living with Lupus for You and Your Family by Robert H. Phillips, Ph.D. (Garden City Park, NY: Avery Publishing Group, Inc., 1991). This book focuses on the emotional aspects of living with lupus. Dr. Phillips, a psychologist, devotes entire chapters to different emotions (fear, anger, guilt) and offers practical advice on coping with those emotions.

The Lupus Book: A Guide for Patients and Their Families by Daniel Wallace, M.D. (NY: Oxford University Press, 1996). Written by one of the world's leading experts on the treatment of lupus, this useful guide offers information on symptoms and causes of the disease, along with a history of lupus and its treatment. The book features fact-filled chapters on how and why lupus affects different organ systems in the body, how lupus affects different age groups, and how patients can take an active role in the management of their illness.

Lupus: Everything You Need to Know by Robert G. Lahita, M.S., and Robert H. Phillips, Ph.D. (Garden City Park, NY: Avery Publishing Group, Inc., 1998). This book provides answers to common questions about systemic lupus erythematosus—its possible causes, symptoms, and treatments. The authors are two of the best-known experts internationally in treatment and coping strategies for lupus.

Web sites

Hamline University Lupus Home Page
http://www.hamline.edu/lupus/

This Web site offers lots of general information (research updates, drug information, etc.) about lupus. The site also includes electronic news groups and mailing lists, links to other organizations, and information on special issues including systemic involvement (skin, kidneys), depression, and more.

Pediatric Rheumatology Home Page
See listing under "Arthritis Resources" on page 93.

Part 2

Learning to Cope

Five Steps for Managing Your Illness

"You have to accept whatever comes and the only important thing is that you meet it with courage and with the best you have to give."
Eleanor Roosevelt

You may wonder if there's a secret to facing life with a chronic illness. There really isn't; nor is there a magic potion that will make your illness disappear forever. Adjusting to life with a chronic illness isn't easy, and it will take hard work on your part. But if you care enough about your body and yourself, you can accept your situation, find the courage that's inside you, and make the most of your life. If you catch yourself thinking "I can't do it," repeat one phrase to yourself: "It's MY life." You can learn to cope because it's your life. You didn't choose to have a chronic illness, but *you* set the rules for how you're going to deal with it.

Okay, so it's your life—now what? You can start following the Five Steps for Managing Your Illness. It may take some time to get used to these strategies and make them work for you. But with a little practice, they'll soon be second nature, and you'll have the tools you need to deal with your chronic illness.

Step #1: Face Your Fears

The diagnosis of a chronic illness can make you feel many different emotions, and the most common of these is usually fear. It's scary to know that chronic illnesses have no known cure and don't follow a set course. Doctors often have trouble predicting how your illness will affect you months, years—even days—from now. At times, your doctor will make an educated guess about the treatment that will work for you; you'll have to wait and see whether the guess is correct.

Fear of your illness can make it much harder for you to cope. Fear weighs you down, causes stress and anxiety, and may prevent you from enjoying the positive aspects of your life. Being afraid can also make you angry. When you're scared about your diagnosis, the symptoms, and what will happen to you in the future, it becomes very difficult to see beyond your illness. To move on with your life, you have to face your fears.

First, try to understand what's causing your fear. One thing that really scared me was all the uncertainty. *What am I going to do? How is my life going to change? What will happen to me?* The questions spun around in my head, and there were no easy answers.

It's human nature to fear new experiences. If your family has ever moved, you understand how scary change can be. You probably wondered if you'd ever make new friends, learn your way around the new neighborhood, or adjust to a different school. Over time, you got used to your new home—maybe it even felt like you'd been there forever. In much the same way, you'll learn to feel "at home" with your chronic illness. As you adjust to the change, you'll make new friends, just like someone who moves to a new town. Many of these friends will probably be doctors and other health professionals— or maybe even people your age with the same illness. You'll get used to your new schedule of taking medication or following a special diet. When you become comfortable with your illness, you'll know that it has become part of your everyday life.

One way to control your fear of the unknown is to learn some basic facts about your illness. How? Ask your doctor questions: "What symptoms should I expect?" "What treatment is best for me?" "What are the common side effects of my treatment?" "What's the square root of 144?" (I like to sneak that one in to see if my doctor is paying attention!) Read about your illness by checking out books from the library, exploring the World Wide Web (if you have access to the Internet), or contacting national organizations involved with your illness.*

It's often said that knowledge is power. By educating yourself, you'll increase your ability to take an active role in managing your illness. You have a right—and a responsibility—to understand what's happening inside of your own body.

Step #2: Be Good to Yourself

It's easy to fall into the habit of dwelling on your illness. *What if I get really sick? What if I die? Why me?* Maybe you're wondering what you did to deserve such a horrible illness or why you're being "punished." Give yourself a break and stop thinking such negative thoughts. You didn't do anything to cause your illness, and it's a waste of time to wonder what "might happen" to you. Although your illness may be hard to accept, you can't change it—so focus instead on how you're going to handle it.

After eleven years of managing my illness, I now know that nothing can happen—tomorrow, the next day, or in the future—that I can't face. It's possible that, in the next few hours, I'll become very sick and have to go to the hospital. If so, I'll deal with it, but until then, I'll continue to live each day and look forward to

---

*This book contains listings of books, Web sites, and organizations for specific illnesses and general health issues. Check the index under "Books," "Web sites," "Organizations," or a specific illness to find what you need.

tomorrow. Being good to yourself means living your life. Promise yourself that you won't give up. Though life has brought you something unexpected, don't stop pursuing your dreams. Dreams are what make each day worth living.

Being good to yourself also means staying positive. Don't drown yourself in negative thoughts and worry. Instead, focus on things that lift your spirits (a hobby, your family and friends, your pet, a walk in the fresh air).

Step #3: Know Your Limits

There's a difference between knowing your limits and limiting yourself. When you *limit yourself,* you hold yourself back from doing things that you really want to do. You may end up hiding in the house all day because you're afraid that if you step outside, you'll get sick or be teased. You refuse to try new things because, after all, how can a "sick person" be expected to live a "normal" life? Think about inspirational stories on the TV news: Did you ever see one where the newscaster said, "Up next, the inspiring story of a person who, because of a chronic illness, gave up on life and has never succeeded at anything"? I didn't think so.

When you *know your limits* and respect them, you're taking an active role in managing your illness. You're deciding not to push yourself harder than you know your body can go. Take some time to get to know the patterns of your illness. Maybe you get tired in the late afternoons and need a rest; perhaps you have a strict medication schedule or a special diet that you need to follow. Eventually, you'll become familiar with your body's needs, and you'll know what you should or shouldn't do.

New limits can be hard to accept. For example, one of my limits is that I have to get at least six hours of sleep every night, or I'll be sick the next day—guaranteed. As you may know, when you're studying for a big test or writing a research paper at the last minute, it's common to stay up late trying to get all of your work done. In college, I couldn't "pull an all-nighter" because I knew that I'd get sick if I did. I had to learn to prepare for tests and papers far in advance and to use my time wisely (that often meant studying while my friends went to movies and other social events). I knew that I had to take care of myself or I'd end up missing even more social opportunities because I'd be in bed with a fever and stomach pain.

Once you know your limits, you can learn to work around them and still accomplish your goals and have fun. Sometimes you may have to find creative solutions for coping with your limitations. Say, for example, that you're supposed to avoid contact sports—this doesn't mean you should forget physical activities altogether. Instead of playing basketball, you might join a swim team, learn to golf, or take up jogging. If you'll be missing class because of your illness, find out if your school has a homebound program so a teacher can work with you one-on-one at your home. If your friends want to go out for pizza but you're not feeling up to it, invite them over to your house; you can have a pizza delivered and rent a few movies instead. These options may not always seem convenient at the time, but your health is your #1 priority.

Step #4: Focus on What You *Can* Do

Look for ways to excel. What are your strengths or talents? Do you love to sing, dance, act, debate, draw, or write? Get involved in activities that allow you to explore your interests and maybe even show off a little. Try a new hobby, start a fun exercise program, or do anything that makes you feel good about yourself. When you focus on what you *can* do, you'll have a better chance of staying positive and of bouncing back when things don't go your way.

If you're feeling down, helping someone else just might make you feel better. Get involved with a community service club at your school or see if your local hospital has a volunteer program. You can also come up with volunteer projects on your own—help an elderly neighbor plant a garden, offer to baby-sit for free for a working mom, or do some odd jobs around your house or neighborhood. When you perform a service for another person, you can't help but forget your own troubles for a while.

Step #5: Express Your Feelings

Having a chronic illness is a big deal (duh!), but you may meet some people who act like it isn't. No matter what others may say, you're going through a lot, and you have a right to feel a mix of emotions—anger, sadness, fear, embarrassment, frustration, confusion, anxiety, resentment, and more. You'll also experience a sense of triumph and accomplishment as you successfully manage your illness or achieve your personal goals. Some days you'll feel great; others will be difficult. This is all perfectly normal because a chronic illness can be an emotional roller-coaster ride.

I remember an awful experience in high school, when I stumbled across a cartoon that someone I considered a friend had drawn of me. At the time, I was being treated with steroid medication, which gave my face a puffy, swollen look. The cartoon showed a person with a huge, round head, a moon face, and a stupid smile. I was horrified and so embarrassed that I barely spoke to anyone for days. Finally, one of my close friends asked me what was going on, and I told her what had happened. She gave me a big hug and told me that I had real friends who would always be there to help me get through my difficulties. I felt a lot better after that.

Don't put your painful feelings aside and act as if they don't exist or bottle them up until you feel like you might explode. Express your emotions. It's healthy to talk about your feelings with a parent, sibling, friend, teacher, doctor, clergy member, or anyone else you trust.

Even if you're not having serious problems, letting out your emotions is a good release. You might try keeping a journal—you'd be surprised at how much better you'll feel after writing your thoughts on paper. (Think of it as taking something that's inside you and putting it in your journal for safekeeping.) You don't have to limit your writings to how you feel about your illness. Describe anything . . . friends, daydreams, romantic interests, places you'd like to go, memories.

If it's hard to get started on your journal, try using the following lines as a springboard for your own ideas:

Journal

My illness makes me feel . . .

I think of myself as . . .

Some things that are hard to deal with are . . .

I can help myself feel better by . . .

Sometimes I worry about . . .

I wish . . .

Check It Out

A Book of Your Own: Keeping a Diary or Journal
by Carla Stevens (NY: Clarion Books, 1993).
This helpful book includes practical suggestions
for keeping a journal, plus excerpts from
diaries past and present.

▲▼▲▼▲▼▲▼▲▼▲▼▲▼

Anne Frank: The Diary of a Young Girl
by Anne Frank (NY: Bantam, 1993). One of the most
famous journals in history is the World War II diary
of Anne Frank. Anne, a young Jewish girl who hid
for years in a secret room to avoid capture by the
Nazis, kept a journal to help her get through an
extremely difficult situation. Her diary was a
private place for her to express the vast range of
emotions she experienced.

▲▼▲▼▲▼▲▼▲▼▲▼▲▼

Anne Frank Online
http://www.annefrank.com/
View a photo essay about Anne Frank's life, read
excerpts from her diary, and learn about the
Anne Frank Center USA.

If you aren't comfortable talking about your feelings or writing them down, there are other ways to express yourself. Maybe you prefer to relax and let go of your emotions by playing or listening to music, drawing or painting, or doing physical activities like dancing, running, or swimming. Meditation is another good alternative.

Sometimes your feelings may be so painful that you become depressed. Depression is serious, and you'll need to find help right away. Signs of depression include anxiety, sadness, anger, confusion, helplessness, hopelessness, and the feeling that your life is completely out of control. If you experience extreme and uncomfortable changes—in your moods, behaviors, or feelings—talk to someone you trust right away. Reach out to a parent, teacher, school counselor, clergy member, or your doctor; these adults may be able to help you find a counselor or psychologist who specializes in helping young people. Don't feel bad about seeking professional help for depression. It's very common for people with chronic illnesses to become depressed as a result of the physical and emotional difficulties in their lives.

If you're depressed and considering suicide, please get *immediate* help. Talk to an adult you trust *now,* but if that isn't an option, look under "Suicide Prevention" in your local phone book. Most cities and many towns have suicide prevention hotlines that are staffed twenty-four hours a day, seven days a week. Check under "Community Services" or look for hotline numbers in your Yellow Pages.

Get Help

The following hotline can offer help
when you need it most:

Covenant House Nineline
1-800-999-9999
http://www.covenanthouse.org
Covenant House provides immediate crisis intervention,
support, and referrals for young people and adults who
are suicidal or in crisis.

Helping Your Doctor Help You

"Don't defy the diagnosis, try to defy the verdict."
Norman Cousins

You may wonder what I could possibly tell you about *your* relationship with *your* doctor. You see her and tell her how you feel. Sometimes she gives you medical tests. Sometimes she prescribes medication and gives you instructions for taking it; you follow them and go back to see your doctor when you feel sick again. That's about it, right? Actually, there's more to it.

When you develop a strong, positive relationship with your doctor, you're taking a more active role in managing your illness. A good relationship with your doctor not only makes you feel better emotionally but also helps your doctor to help you. Believe it or not, many people with chronic illnesses think of their doctors as friends. Don't get me wrong—you probably won't be going to the movies together, but you *can* have a good relationship. Making this happen is mostly up to you.

I remember feeling frustrated with doctors who didn't take the time to get to know anything about me as a person. They would come in, look at my medical chart, ask me a bunch of questions, then send me away with five new kinds of pills and an appointment to come back in three weeks. I felt as if I were being interrogated: "You say you've been having fevers. How high? How often? Well, would you say twice a week? Daily? Okay, and that stomach pain, where exactly is it? Do you ever have any pain here? When do you get the pain? In the morning, at night, both, or constantly? Does it happen about an hour after you eat?" I'd look to my mom, hoping she could help me recall the patterns of my illness and how long my symptoms had been present. I'd leave the doctor's office feeling annoyed and frustrated—the doctor was supposed to tell *me* what was wrong, not the other way around . . . or so I thought. Eventually, I came to realize that it was in my own best interests to play a more active role in my treatment and medical appointments.

A Positive Attitude Can Help

If you go to your doctor's office with a negative, resentful attitude ("Okay, I'm here. Heal me!"), you'll probably leave feeling as if you have no control over your medical treatment. You may even think of your doctor as the enemy. However, if you arrive at your appointments ready to share and learn information about your illness, you'll probably feel as if you and your doctor are partners working toward the same goal—to make you as healthy as possible.

Take a moment to think about how you view your doctor. As a friend? A dictator? Someone you trust and respect? Someone you fear? These are all natural emotions. Try to see your doctor as one player on a team dedicated to helping you manage your illness. *You* are a very important part of this team, too. The success of your team depends on all of its members participating to the best of their abilities.

Your doctor's role on your health-care team is to diagnose your illness, prescribe medications, monitor your progress, and adjust your treatments when necessary. Your doctor isn't a fortune-teller who can answer the question "When am I going to feel better?" Your doctor isn't superhuman, either—she can't give you a magic pill that will make all of your symptoms disappear (such pills don't exist for people who have chronic health problems—not yet, anyway!). Chronic illness is frustrating not only for you but also for your doctor. She wants you to feel better and will do her best to make that happen, but the treatments aren't always successful.

As the patient, you have your own set of responsibilities. In fact, the word "patient" can help you remember some ways to make your relationship with your doctor a success.

Prepare for doctor visits.

Ask questions about things that you don't understand.

Tell your doctor how you feel.

Inquire about new medications and products.

Explain your symptoms.

Notice how you feel.

Try to follow the doctor's advice and instructions.

Your illness isn't simple. While the mystery of what's wrong with you was settled with your diagnosis, you'll continue to encounter smaller mysteries (new symptoms, which medications work and why) as your illness unfolds and as you search for better treatments. A key part of solving these mysteries is being a careful observer of your own health between visits to the doctor.

What to Do *Before* Your Appointment

Your doctor visits will go more smoothly if you write down the patterns of your illness as they happen. That way, you'll be able to answer the doctor's questions about your symptoms, reactions to medications, side effects, and other issues. One tool for remembering your illness patterns is a Symptom Journal. You can use a notebook or a diary, or keep your Symptom Journal on your computer—whatever works for you. Your journal can help your doctor see patterns that may help solve the mystery of how best to treat you.

You don't have to write a detailed description of every symptom and side effect—just enough to help you remember how you were feeling and when. When you're at the doctor's office, you can refer to the journal anytime your doctor asks a question.

Keep your journal with you whenever possible. If you don't want to carry it with you all the time or stop what you're doing to jot down how you feel, just make a mental note to write things down as soon as you can.

Journal

Tuesday, June 22 11:50 A.M.

Slight fever (99.8°).
Pain in lower right part of stomach.
7 P.M. Fever again (100°).
Not hungry.

Saturday, June 26 11 A.M.

Fever (99.7°). Feel sick to stomach.
No pain.
8:30 P.M. Tired. Not hungry.
Mild fever (99.8°).

Monday, June 28

12 P.M. Tired. Muscles ache.
Pain in upper right stomach.

◀ List Your Medications ▶

It's helpful to have a list of your current medications available when you're at the doctor's office. You may think, "But why? My doctor is the one who prescribed them for me." Keep in mind that your doctor sees a variety of patients all day long. By keeping a list of your medications and doses handy (your Symptom Journal is a good place for this), you'll save your doctor the time of having to look through your chart. That gives your doctor a few more minutes to talk with you about your treatment.

To make the list even more useful, record whether any of the medications are making you sick or if you're experiencing side effects, such as nausea, fatigue, rashes, or weight gain. If you think that a certain medication is causing serious side effects, plan to ask your doctor about alternatives that you could try.

◀ Learn Everything You Can ▶ About Your Illness

To find answers about your illness, you need to learn everything you can about its symptoms and treatments. Most medical offices have basic pamphlets and brochures on the illnesses they treat; the national organizations* that produce the materials will usually include their names, addresses, and phone numbers on the back so you can get more information. You can also check out books from your library or, if you have access to the Internet, you can go online and conduct a search using the name of your illness.

As you discover more about your illness, you'll probably have lots of questions about your symptoms, treatments, side effects, or how you feel in general. You may also have questions about new medications or procedures you've researched. When you see your doctor, ask questions—each one brings you that much closer to

---

*For more on national organizations, see "Support Groups and National Organizations," pp. 176–184.

understanding your illness. Since you probably won't remember every question that pops into your head, write them down in your Symptom Journal as they occur to you. Don't get carried away, though. Your doctor probably won't react well to you storming into her office, shoving your journal in her face, and shouting: "Ah-ha! Isn't it true that THIS medication has fewer side effects than the one you prescribed, *Doctor?*" Play it cool; you and your doctor are on the same side.

◀ Find an Appointment Buddy ▶

If you're not old enough to drive or if you're very sick, you'll need to have someone take you to your appointments—usually a parent. Even if you're old enough to get to the doctor's office on your own, you may want to consider bringing someone (a parent, relative, or friend) along anyway. The person who accompanies you to the doctor's office can act as your regular Appointment Buddy.

Appointment Buddies are a great source of emotional support. When you're waiting for test results, for example, it's comforting to have someone there to talk about how you're feeling. An Appointment Buddy can also help you remember what the doctor says because you may not recall everything (especially if you're upset about test results). Best of all, your Appointment Buddy can help you keep things in perspective and let you know that you're not alone.

◀ Bring Something to Do ▶

They don't call it a "waiting room" for no reason. As you probably know, doctor appointments usually involve time spent waiting and staring at the clock. The selection of magazines in the office may not interest you, so why not have something to keep you occupied while you wait? Bring a hand-held video game or a tape player with headphones. Better yet, use the free time to get your home-work done. Keeping busy can help relieve your anxiety.

Making the Most of Your Appointment

By communicating openly about your symptoms, side effects, and concerns, you'll be making the most of time spent with your doctor. Ask questions from your list and be sure to write down the answers. If your doctor uses words or terms that you haven't heard before, ask what they mean. Don't be afraid to interrupt—just be polite about it.

How NOT to ask questions:

Hold it right there. What the heck is all this about more tests?

Try this instead:

I'm sorry to interrupt, but I'm not sure what these new tests are for. Could you please tell me?

How NOT to raise a concern:

I'm sick of this medication. It makes me want to throw up, and I'm not going to take it anymore.

Try this instead:

I've had problems with nausea ever since I've been taking this medication. I'd really like to see if we can find one that doesn't cause this kind of side effect.

Don't feel embarrassed to ask questions about your medications or treatment. Doctors deal with medical issues every day and sometimes may forget that their patients don't automatically understand everything. Your doctor relies on your help and feedback to find the best medical treatment for you.

Part of working on a team is being a good listener, too. Your doctor may tell you about an upcoming test or procedure, or explain a change in your treatment. Your job is not only to listen but also to *understand* what the doctor says. Write things down and ask as many questions as you need to (your Appointment Buddy can speak up, too).

◀ Explain Your Symptoms and Feelings ▶

Your doctor will need specific information to help design a treatment plan that works for you. Your treatment will be more successful if you're honest about how you feel—not only physically (where it hurts and how long it's been hurting) but also emotionally (whether you're adjusting to your treatment). Sometimes I didn't like the side effects of my medication, but instead of being honest about it, I'd just tell my doctor that I felt a lot better so she'd take me off the medication. This meant that I was going off my medication too soon, which wasn't fair to my doctor or to me. I ended up feeling even worse.

If you don't like a certain medication or method of treatment, talk to your doctor about alternatives. Maybe you'll even have suggestions for new treatments, based on reading you've done or talks you've had with other people who have the same illness. What works for someone else may not work for you, but it doesn't hurt to try other options. Keep at it until you find one that works.

If you're very upset about your illness, talk to your doctor instead of hiding your feelings. Your doctor may be able to recommend a counselor or psychologist to help you deal with your painful emotions, or perhaps can refer you to a support group* of people your age with similar health issues. You don't have to manage your illness all alone—ask for help when you need it.

---

*For more on support groups, see "Support Groups and National Organizations," pp. 176–184.

What to Do *After* Your Appointment

After your appointment, compare notes with your Appointment Buddy. Did you both hear the same things? If you have conflicting information, figure out why. You may have to make a follow-up call to your doctor to get the information straight.

Once you've reviewed the visit, think about what you need to do until your next appointment. Follow your doctor's instructions and advice as closely as possible. If you're not supposed to take your medication on an empty stomach, eat a snack first. If you're supposed to avoid the sun, don't spend two hours tanning. Sometimes you may feel limited by the things you're not allowed to do—that's natural. But if you ignore your doctor's advice, you're fighting your own body and hurting your chances of feeling better. Doctors get frustrated when their patients do things that are self-defeating; as a team player, take responsibility for following the plan that you and your doctor have agreed on.

Is It Time to Change Doctors?

What if you do everything you can to be a team player and you're still not happy with your relationship with your doctor? It's possible that you and your doctor just aren't a good fit. Maybe you think you spend too much time in the waiting room, that your questions aren't addressed, or that you're not getting enough information about new treatments. Your doctor has a responsibility to put some effort into your relationship and, as a patient, you have the right to a doctor who:

◆ listens and tries to answer your questions

◆ doesn't ask you to wait more than forty-five minutes for each appointment

◆ is willing to discuss different treatment options

◆ learns about new research and developments in the treatment of your illness.

If your doctor isn't meeting your needs, compare notes to see if your Appointment Buddy agrees. If so, it may be time to change doctors. Your doctor should be someone you're comfortable with and have confidence in. What do you do when it's time to "break up" with your doctor? Try not to feel anxious about it. Keep your rights in mind and remember that you've done all you can to make the relationship work.

There are many ways to find a new doctor. You can start by asking your current doctor for a *referral,* or recommendation of another qualified physician. If you don't feel comfortable doing this, perhaps your parents will approach your doctor for you. Another option is talking to other people who have the same illness and asking for their suggestions. Or you can call a national organization* dedicated to your illness to find the names of doctors in your area. Just be sure that the doctor you choose is a match with your health insurance plan.

▲ ▼▲▼▲▼▲▼

A good relationship with your doctor is an essential part of dealing with your illness positively. By taking an active role in the relationship and in your treatment, you're taking the best possible care of yourself.

---

*For more on national organizations, see "Support Groups and National Organizations," pp. 176–184.

Telling Your Friends and Classmates

"Each person's life is lived as a series of conversations."
Deborah Tannen

One of the hardest parts about learning that you have a chronic illness is telling your friends and peers. At first, it was too painful for me to think about revealing my "horrible secret" to even my closest friends. I hid my disease for years. Once I finally told them, however, I discovered that being honest about my illness was easier than trying to pretend that it didn't exist.

Not knowing for sure how people might react to your news is probably the scariest part. The uncertainty can drive you crazy. *What will they say if I tell them? I think they'll react okay, but what if they don't? What if people think I'm a freak? Will I have any friends anymore?* Uncertainty is part of life (chronic illness or not), and you need to accept that some things are out of your control. But there are ways to make breaking the news much easier for you and the people you tell.

Who to Tell

Your friends are the people who, in many ways, know you better than anyone else in the world. You're used to sharing things with them, but your illness is BIG. This kind of information is a lot different from news about your latest crush or how you scored on the recent math test. Ultimately, who you tell is up to you. You may choose to tell all of your classmates, or you may decide to confide in only a few close friends.

Some illnesses are easier to hide than others. If you have an illness like diabetes and have to do something highly noticeable, such as test your blood or give yourself insulin injections, it may be easier in the long run to tell all of your classmates, fellow members of clubs and sports teams, and anyone else you see on a regular basis. This way, you're avoiding the discomfort that comes with trying to hide something relatively obvious (it's like trying to throw a blanket over an elephant—people are going to know something's up). If you have more of a "secret illness," where the symptoms, treatments, and side effects aren't very noticeable, you can choose to be more selective about telling people you know.

How to Tell

Once you've decided who to tell, it's time to figure out how you're going to tell them. You don't have to sit down and plot an elaborate strategy (this isn't war), but you *are* up against a formidable opponent—uncertainty. Because you can't be sure how people will react, the best plan of action is to tell them in a way that feels comfortable and honest.

Avoid the "drop the bomb" approach:

Hi! Can I talk to you? I think you should sit down. Okay, I'm just going to come out and say it, and I hope that you're not grossed out or anything. I have a chronic disease. It's really weird because no one knows why you get it and there's no cure, and sometimes I can't eat regular food, and I'll have to take medication that will make my face all puffy, and I'll get really bad pain in my stomach and might have to have surgery. I can handle it all, though, and I'm sure you can, too.

How would you react to something like that? You'd probably feel overwhelmed and confused by what you've just heard. It's good to get things out in the open, but saying too much too fast can make your friends feel like a bomb has been dropped in their lap.

The "dump and run" approach isn't great either:

I really need to get this off my chest, so here goes: I have a chronic illness, and it makes me have a lot of symptoms and see the doctor a lot. But that's life. Whew! I'm glad I got that out. Thanks for listening. You're a real friend, you know? Now I have to get to history class before all of the good seats are taken. See ya!

This approach is especially tempting when you're telling a larger group of people, instead of just one friend, because you get it over with quickly and don't have to wait around for questions. When you spill your guts and disappear, however, no one has time to let the news sink in or to adjust to what you've just told them. You may give people the impression that you don't want to answer any questions or explain further.

No matter how many people you're talking to, *you* control how you present the information. You can tell them about your illness calmly and effectively. Whether you plan to tell just one friend or a whole group of people, practice what you're going to say. Write it down and rehearse the words in front of a mirror until you feel comfortable. You could even do a test run with a parent or friend who already knows about your illness. Each time you tell someone, it will get easier.

You'll probably be nervous because telling people about your illness is a big deal, but don't rush through your explanations. Speak slowly to make sure that you're understood. People will probably be surprised by what you tell them, and they'll take their cues for how to react from you. If you seem calm and accepting, they'll probably respond in kind. Remember to just be honest. There's a reason why you're telling your friends—you need their support. Life with a chronic illness isn't easy, and you want to convey that truthfully. If you say things like "It's not that bad," you may give people the impression that you don't really need their help and support. They may not realize that you have certain needs and limitations as a result of your illness.

With my illness (Crohn's disease), it's common to go through at least one operation, maybe more. I knew that I had to tell people not only about my symptoms but also about the likelihood of surgery. That way, my friends could be prepared for what might happen to me. You don't have to include all the graphic details of your illness (most people probably aren't ready to hear about how many times you were in the bathroom or other such, well . . . *personal* matters). Just be clear about your symptoms, medications, side effects, doctor visits, medical tests, and other important facts.

When you let people know about your illness, keep in mind *who* you're talking to. Depending on whether you're telling a close friend or a group of people, you can choose how detailed your explanation will be. Classmates or fellow team members may need only basic information, such as how your illness will affect your life at school. It's up to you how much to share beyond that. Go slowly, though, to get a sense of people's reactions. If they seem open and you'd like to tell them more, go ahead. You may choose to share more detailed and private information only with close friends.

Once your friends know, they can support you if you're preparing to tell a larger group.

Expect people to have questions—after all, you probably had a lot of questions when you first found out about your illness, and other people will be no different. They may not ask right away, so let them know that if they have any questions—whether it's days, weeks, or even months later—they can always come to you, and you'll do your best to answer them. Some people may not ask any questions at all; in fact, their reaction may be dead silence. Don't be discouraged if people are quiet when they hear your news—they may be surprised or unsure about what to say. If they just stare at you after you tell them, it won't help matters if you burst into tears or get angry. Their reaction doesn't mean they're rejecting you.

Your friends and classmates will let you know when they're ready to talk further about your illness. Some may respond immediately, giving you all the support you need; others may shy away from you at first, but hopefully they'll learn to adjust. Leave the door open and be patient. More often than not, your true friends will stand by you, and other people will be as supportive as they can. Being honest about your illness is a sign of the trust and faith that you have in people, and they need to know how much you value their friendship, encouragement, and support.

True friends won't stop liking you because of your illness. If someone decides to stop being friends with you because of your news, you're better off without that person in your life. If this happens and you feel hurt and rejected, talk to your real friends about the situation. Let them be a source of comfort.

▲▼▲▼▲▼▲▼

Given all of these tips, here's a good way to tell someone about your chronic illness:

I'd like to talk to you about something important—do you have some time right now? You've probably noticed that I haven't really been myself lately. I think of you as a good friend, and I want you to know what's going on in my life. I went to the doctor last week and found out that I have something called Crohn's disease. Have you ever heard of it? It can be a serious illness, and I'd like to tell you a little about it. I know this is probably a big surprise. It was for me, too.

Crohn's disease affects the digestive system. You know that I've been having a lot of pain in my stomach—it's because I have an infection that was caused by the Crohn's. They're not sure why some people get Crohn's disease, and there's no known cure. I'll be taking medication, but there's a chance it won't work. If that happens, I might have to have surgery to remove the infection.

I'm going to have this disease for the rest of my life, but that doesn't mean I'll always be sick. For long periods of time I'll probably be healthy, but at other times I won't feel good. Then I won't be able to go out or eat certain foods. I know that this is a lot of new information, and it will take a little getting used to, but I want you to know that if you ever have any questions, you can ask me. I want you to feel that you can talk to me about it at any time.

You can modify this approach to suit your particular illness and the people you're telling, but the same basic rules apply. Be honest. Don't act as if your illness is no big deal. At the same time, don't scare people by going into graphic details. If they want to know those things, they'll ask when they're ready. Explain that their support matters to you, which is why you're telling them about your illness.

Once you face the fear and uncertainty that comes with talking about your illness, you'll gain more confidence. Eventually, opening up will become second nature, and you'll feel comfortable approaching the topic and answering questions. As more of your friends become aware of your illness, you'll be surrounded by people who understand and care about you. This support system can make life with a chronic illness much easier.

You and Your Family

"Pain nourishes courage. You can't be brave if you've only had wonderful things happen to you."
Mary Tyler Moore

When you were diagnosed with a chronic illness, your life wasn't the only one that changed. Your entire family has had to deal with the changes, too; chronic illness has now become a part of *their* lives. Whether you live with two parents or one, or are being raised by a grandparent or guardian, whether you have brothers and sisters or are an only child, the people closest to you are affected by your illness. Your diagnosis can make them feel scared, frustrated, and even resentful.

The diagnosis of a chronic illness is a stressful event for a family, and living with illness on a daily basis has a huge effect on family life. Everyone's role in the family suddenly changes, and the focus is now mainly on *you* (whether you want it to be or not). It's like you're suddenly walking on a tightrope, and your family is waiting below, hoping they'll be able to catch you if you fall.

Each family member faces different issues while adjusting to these changes. You may see a mix of anger, confusion, uncertainty, and sadness. Your family may have trouble getting used to your special needs; they may even resent their responsibility of helping you manage your illness. Don't feel guilty, though. These are all natural emotions, and none of them are your fault. It's up to you, however, to help your family adjust to your illness. To do this, you need to understand what each person may be feeling.

If you're thinking, "Why should *I* help *them* when I'm the one who's suffering the most?" here's the answer: You'll feel better, and so will they. Your family can be your greatest lifelong source of strength and support as you deal with your illness. If you're there for them, chances are they'll be there for you, too. You may even find that chronic illness brings all of you closer together.

There are two keys to helping your family adjust to your illness:

1. Take an active role in managing your illness.

2. Open the lines of communication with family members.

When you take an active role in your illness, you'll help put everyone in your family more at ease. Gradually, they'll grow accustomed to your new routines and see that you can take care of yourself. If you show them that you're comfortable talking about your illness, they'll be more likely to open up and communicate themselves. Talking honestly about your needs and fears and listening to how others are dealing with things is a great way to build mutual support. Encourage your family members to talk about their feelings and to tell you what they need from you. At first, it may seem as if all anyone talks about is your illness, but soon it will be just one more aspect of your family's life.

Your Parents

Your parents will probably feel shocked and sad after hearing your diagnosis. They most likely never expected you to have a chronic illness, and they'll wonder what your future will be like. Because they hope for the best for you and want you to live a happy, healthy life, they may also feel very scared. You're in a situation that your parents can't fix or rescue you from—they can't protect you from your illness. All of these feelings conflict with your parents' need to be strong and to help you and the rest of the family get through this difficult time.

What do many parents do when they're worried about their children? They become more protective. Your response may be to get angry and say that they're treating you like a baby. The problems are doubled because you rely on your parents to help manage your medical care. Depending on the severity of your illness, there may be times when you're too sick to take care of yourself and need your parents' help more than ever. This can be very frustrating and make you feel as if you'll never have a chance to grow up.

If you think that your parents are being overprotective, take a moment to consider what they're going through. They're worried about your health and safety. They're afraid for you, and they want to do what's best for you. I remember when I was little and wanted to walk to school by myself; at first, my mom said no and continued walking me to school, holding my hand all the way. One day, finally, she let me go on my own. She stood in the driveway as I walked off to school, and every few steps, I turned around to see if she was still standing there watching me. She was. Finally, I'd gone so far that when I turned around, I could no longer see our house or my mom. Now that I think about it, she must have been really scared to let go. Once you understand how your parents are feeling, it becomes easier to talk to them about your needs. They may not realize that you want some breathing room, but how are they supposed to know if you don't tell them?

I remember a situation that occurred during my senior year of high school over winter break, two weeks after I had surgery. I was still weak and slept on the couch for most of the day. One of my best friends down the street was going to have a party, and I really wanted to go and see everyone. I thought it would make me feel better to be with my friends, but because of my illness and recent hospital visit, my parents didn't want me to go. We reached a compromise—I could go to the party for one hour, and I had to rest all day to conserve my energy for the evening. It worked out well because I felt tired after an hour anyway, and the party really did cheer me up.

When you want to be independent despite your illness, your parents may be nervous—but only because they care so much about you. If your illness is new to them, they may doubt that you can handle it. Show your parents that you can manage your illness responsibly, and they'll learn to trust that you can take care of yourself. They'll come to see that you're aware of your abilities and your limitations. They may realize that they don't have to worry about you quite so much (well, okay—they'll still worry, they'll just hide it better!).

If your parents are reluctant to let you make your own choices, ask them why. Demonstrate each day that you're responsible enough to handle your illness. Once they see that you're able to make good decisions, your parents will realize that you're able to take care of yourself. (Be reasonable, though. Don't expect your parents to let you drop out of school or hitchhike across the country just because you asked nicely.)

◀ Communicating with Parents ▶

When you're feeling angry, talk with your parents—but don't unleash your anger on them. Whenever I got mad about a decision my parents had made, I'd yell at my father, and he'd always say, "Well, if you're going to talk to me like that, the answer is definitely NO." Sound familiar?

Looking back on it, we were having trouble communicating. Good communication is essential in all families because it's the first step in solving problems. If I'd been able to talk calmly about my feelings, instead of yelling about how unfair my parents were, I probably would have avoided many conflicts. At first, it may not feel comfortable to sit down and talk about your feelings and needs, but the more you do it, the easier it will get. Following are some tips for effective communication with your parents:

How NOT to express your feelings:

I'm really sick of having this illness. I feel terrible. Why did I have to be born this way? It's all your fault!

Blaming only makes everyone feel worse, and it's nobody's fault that you have a chronic illness. People will be more willing to listen if you explain your feelings calmly.

Try this instead:

I'm frustrated and angry because I don't feel well, and it's hard to think about living with this illness for the rest of my life. I need to be alone right now, but I'd like to talk to you about things later.

If you use this approach, your parents will be more likely to understand and accept what you're feeling. Invite your parents to talk with you later, after you've had time to calm down.

How NOT to ask for favors:

Whenever I want to do something, you say no. You're being a jerk, and I'm just going to do what I want no matter what you say.

You're a lot less likely to get what you want when you talk to your parents this way. Call me crazy, but using the words "you" and "jerk" in the same sentence probably isn't the best means of persuasion.

Your parents' natural reaction will probably be to get angry and tell you that you aren't mature enough to make your own decisions. Although it may be difficult, remain calm.

Try this instead:

I'd like to talk with you about something. I know you said I can't go out tonight, but I'm not very comfortable with that decision. You said you're worried that I might get sick, but I want you to know that I can handle it. I feel I've shown that I can take care of myself. If I do begin to feel sick, I'll call you. You can trust me. I'd really like to go tonight and would appreciate it if you'd reconsider your decision.

When you talk openly and honestly like this, your parents will see how mature and responsible you are. They'll feel reassured that you really can take care of yourself, and they'll be more likely to support your need to make your own decisions.

Tip

Learning good communication skills takes time. If your efforts to talk with your parents and share your feelings meet with resistance, you may want to consider seeking professional help. A counselor or family therapist may be the answer. Talk to your doctor about how to get in touch with a mental-health professional.

Your Brothers and Sisters

Guess what? Despite being a pain sometimes, your brothers and sisters love you. Your illness will probably have a big impact on them, and they'll worry about your health. They may be scared and uncertain about how your illness will affect you and the entire family. They may also be a little envious if you're suddenly getting a lot of attention from your parents and other important people in your life, as a result of your illness.

Occasionally, your health will take priority over the needs of your brothers and sisters. It's common for your siblings to feel neglected when your parents spend a lot of time taking care of you (bringing you to the doctor, monitoring your medication schedule, talking to you about your symptoms). Your parents may unexpectedly have to drop everything to attend to your needs. For example, they may need to drive you to the hospital, which means they'll miss your little brother's soccer game. The result? Everyone feels bad: Your parents are upset about the missed soccer game (and worried about you), you feel guilty that your illness is causing scheduling problems, and your brother is hurt and angry that your parents can't watch him play *and* feels guilty because he knows that you can't help it that you're sick. Try to understand what your brothers and sisters are going through, and don't be afraid to talk to them about their feelings. Let them know that you care.

If you have older siblings, you may find that they start acting as if they're the parent, babying you because you have an illness. As frustrating as this can be, it's important to remember *why* they're doing this—out of concern for you. They want you to get better and may feel that it's their duty as an older brother or sister to protect you from harm. Although my older sister and I fought when we were younger, she worried a lot about my health after my diagnosis. In fact, I *still* sometimes catch her trying to baby me! If you feel smothered, say so. Tell your brothers and sisters that you appreciate their kindness but can take care of yourself.

Your brothers and sisters may also be afraid that they can't help you when you're sick. This is often the case when your illness is characterized by sudden attacks, such as seizures. Fear can cause your siblings to distance themselves from you. If your sisters and brothers are feeling guilty, angry, or resentful, they may start spending less time with you. Communication is the key to keeping your relationship with your siblings on track. Be open and honest with them whenever possible. Let them know that you understand how they feel and need their care and support.

Younger siblings will probably be confused about your illness. In fact, children under the age of seven may have a tough time understanding the concept of a chronic illness because, in their experience, people get sick but then are all better. An ongoing or periodic illness is more difficult to understand. They may wonder how you can be sick one day but feel fine the next. Worse yet, they may worry that you're going to die. Sometimes younger siblings become convinced that *they* are the cause of the illness. Have you ever wished bad things on people you were mad at? Younger siblings who have done this may believe that something they said caused you to get sick. Reassure your younger brothers and sisters that it's not their fault that you have an illness.

Emotions such as fear, frustration, envy, guilt, and resentment are natural, and the best way to deal with all of these jumbled-up feelings is to talk things out. It may feel awkward at first, especially if you aren't that close to your siblings. In fact, talking about your chronic illness may help you grow closer and understand one another better.

◀ Communicating with Siblings ▶

Negative feelings can result in anger and fights among siblings. If this starts happening at your house, figure out what you can do to help resolve the conflicts. Maybe you need to back off if your sister or brother is really irritable, then try to talk about it later. Don't allow yourself to get drawn into fights—they'll only add more stress to your life. Instead, react calmly and ask what's *really* the matter.

Don't whine or say things like, "How can you treat me this way when I'm so sick?" Let your siblings know that you understand their feelings and try to make peace. When you're communicating with your brothers and sisters, keep some of the following tips in mind:

How NOT to address a problem:

You know, I'm really sick of your pouting. You're so selfish! My doctor appointments are more important than some stupid dance recital.

If you minimize the importance of what's going on in their lives, your brothers and sisters may feel as if you don't care about them. Acknowledge their feelings, then talk about your own.

Try this instead:

I understand that you're upset that Mom and Dad couldn't go to your recital. You must have been really disappointed. I know they would have gone if they could. We all would have. Unfortunately, this was the only time I could get in to see the doctor. I hope we'll be able to plan things a little better in the future so this won't happen again.

When you let your sisters and brothers know that you're trying to see their side of things, they'll be more accepting of the impact your illness has on your family.

Your siblings may be fearful of your illness and how it affects you. Show your brothers and sisters that they don't need to be scared *of* you or *for* you. Help them understand that your illness is manageable and that you probably aren't going to die from it. By learning as much as you can about your illness, you'll be able to explain to your siblings exactly what's happening and why. This knowledge can calm their fears.

Don't try to hide the truth about your illness, either. Your siblings will see that you and your parents are acting differently, and they'll notice that you've been getting sick a lot. Even very young children will appreciate knowing the truth. You may be afraid that telling them will make them more upset, but the fear of *not* knowing is often worse. If you tell your siblings what they can do for you if you get sick, they'll feel more prepared and able to help.

Another important reason for being honest with your siblings is that there's a good chance that their friends or other people in the community will ask them what's wrong with you. If they know the answer, your brothers and sisters won't fear these kinds of questions; they can respond honestly and show people that a chronic illness isn't something to hide.

Allow your siblings to visit you if you're in the hospital or ask them to go with you to your doctor appointments. Your doctor may be able to explain your illness in a way that younger brothers and sisters can understand. Your siblings will feel more involved if they can see firsthand what happens during one of your appointments, and they'll become aware of what it's really like to have a chronic illness. They may no longer resent the attention that you get from your parents, once it's clear how serious the tests and treatments for your illness are. An added bonus is that your sisters and brothers can offer you support while you're at the hospital or doctor's office.

▲▼▲▼▲▼▲▼

Family members can be some of your greatest supporters, but not if you don't give them a chance. Be honest and tell them if you're afraid. Talk about how your doctor appointment went; let them know whether your new medications are helping. Ask your family for what you need, but also be prepared to listen to what *they* need.

Tip

Have a plan of action that everyone in the family is aware of, in case you get sick or have an emergency. Your plan could include:

◆ who to call (a nearby relative, a neighbor, a doctor, or 911)
◆ what symptoms to watch for
◆ how to deal with severe symptoms
◆ a list of medications you're taking and how much of each.

Keep your plan somewhere handy—on the refrigerator, on a family bulletin board, or in a nearby kitchen drawer. Just make sure that everyone knows where it is.

Coping at School

"All things are difficult before they are easy."
Thomas Fuller

School is tough enough without a chronic illness. Not only do you have to deal with classes, homework, relationships, and extracurricular activities, but also your illness and all of its symptoms. On top of all that, you might be going through puberty, which is a difficult time physically and emotionally. These changes are often intensified when you have a chronic illness, making this time of your life more challenging than ever.

Sometimes you may want to blend in with your friends, wearing similar kinds of clothes or participating in the same extracurricular activities. Other times, you may wish to be different—to distinguish yourself. Maybe you'd like to excel in math or English, have a winning experiment in the school science fair, be a knockout goalie, perform the lead role in the school play, or travel to faraway places. You probably never wanted to be different in *this* way, though—the one with the disease.

To survive at school, you need to accept your illness and the challenges it presents. This can be extremely hard to do, but you'll feel a lot better about yourself when you realize that you aren't abnormal, strange, or weird. Once I'd accepted that a chronic illness is normal for me, I gained confidence and felt more comfortable around other people. School became easier.

With some planning, you can minimize (and possibly eliminate) the negative impact that your chronic illness has on your life at school. Think of it as having an Escape Plan—like the kind that the fire department recommends, so you can get away safely if there's a fire. You hope that you'll never need to use your Escape Plan, but it's important to have one if the worst happens. In case you get sick at school or need to be hospitalized, you'll be prepared.

I began to get sick (as a result of my Crohn's disease) in October of my senior year of high school. Because I'd been relatively healthy up to that point, I figured I wasn't in danger of having a flare-up, and I hadn't told many people about my illness. "Why go to the trouble of telling my classmates and teachers?" I thought. When my doctor put me on steroids that made me gain weight and have a swollen, puffy face, people were confused about what was happening to me. This was a very stressful time because, in addition to trying to hide my illness, I was constantly worried about how I was going to keep up with my school work and activities. I didn't have a plan in place, so I had no idea how to cope with my situation. Then my doctor told me that I had to have surgery, and I felt as if my life had gone completely out of control.

I hope that you don't have to deal with a flare-up or hospitalization, but if you do, it's important to have a coping strategy. Part of your plan should be letting other people at school know about your illness and what they can do in case you get really sick. Following are some suggestions for making an Escape Plan that includes informing your school nurse, teachers, school counselor, and other adults you may encounter each day.

The School Nurse

If there's one person at school who should know about your illness, it's the nurse. In fact, the nurse can be one of your closest allies. There may be times when you feel fatigued or sick, or have a flare-up at school. If this happens, rest. Go to the nurse's office and lie down for a while until you feel good enough to return to class. (NOTE: Don't take advantage of this option. It may, for example, look a little suspicious if you start to "feel sick" every time there's a pop quiz in your history class. The nurse and your teachers are trusting you to be honest with them.)

You can create a Care Sheet, a helpful tool for the nurse to keep on file. A Care Sheet includes specific information on the nature and treatment of your illness, as well as what to do in case of an emergency. Be sure to list the phone numbers of your parents, doctor, and other emergency contacts who will know what to do in a crisis. It's a good idea to type the information on a computer (keep a backup copy on disk) so you can easily make changes if you need to. Ask your doctor to take a look at your Care Sheet to make sure that everything is accurate before giving it to the school nurse. On page 162 is a sample Care Sheet that you can use as a reference when creating your own.

Many schools have policies about medications, so look in your school handbook or ask your school nurse to explain the policy. You'll probably need to bring your school nurse a note from your parents or doctor, indicating the times and reasons for taking your medication. Most likely, your school will require you to store your medications at the nurse's office, instead of carrying them with you, because the school is responsible for your safety and that of other students. While it may seem silly to go to the nurse's office each time you need to take a pill, this ensures that no other students can take your medication and that you'll receive the correct dosage.

CARE SHEET FOR JOE BLAKE

Joe Blake has diabetes. He receives insulin twenty-four hours a day through an external insulin pump because his body doesn't produce enough of this hormone. He must eat meals on time and may need a morning and a mid-afternoon snack to balance his daily doses of insulin. *He must be allowed to have a snack whenever he feels the need to eat.*

Joe may have an insulin reaction if his blood sugar is too low (hypoglycemia). A hypoglycemic reaction can be sudden and severe, especially before meals, after exercise, or as a result of stress. He may not realize that an insulin reaction is coming, so it's important for you to be aware of the signs and treatment.

SIGNS:

Sudden mood changes, staring, rapid speech, excessive talking, disjointed speech, confusion, shaking, sweating, pale skin, faintness, nausea, poor coordination, blurred vision, headache.

TREATMENT:

An insulin reaction requires immediate action. Don't leave Joe alone until the symptoms begin to go away. His judgment and coordination may be impaired, and he may lose consciousness. Give him sugar immediately, including one of the following (he carries extra supplies in his backpack): a 6 oz. can of *regular* soda—*not diet,* 1/2 cup fruit juice, three glucose tablets, or two large teaspoons of sugar dissolved in water.

Symptoms should start to go away within ten minutes; if not, repeat the treatment. If symptoms persist after thirty minutes, call Joe's parents or doctor (see phone numbers below).

If Joe is unconscious, having convulsions, or unable to swallow, *call 911 immediately and report a diabetic insulin shock.*

Mrs. Blake at work: 555-7979
Mr. Blake at work: 555-4523
Home phone: 555-9032
Dr. Andrew Reynolds: 555-8485

What do you do if your school doesn't have a nurse on staff? Because many schools don't have a nurse due to budget reasons, you and your parents may have to talk to your principal about your illness and how it affects you at school. Make sure your principal receives a copy of your Care Sheet. Depending on school policy, you may have to ask a teacher or aide to administer your medication. If no teacher is willing to do this, a parent may have to come to school each day and give you your medication.

Your Teachers

Your teachers play a big role in your school life, so it's a good idea to let them know about your illness and how it affects you. You can decide which teachers you want to tell, but I suggest letting all of them know so they're prepared in case you have an emergency. If you don't feel comfortable talking to them directly, see if your parents or the school nurse can explain for you. Make sure that your teachers receive a copy of your Care Sheet so they can react appropriately in an emergency. Many young people with chronic illnesses try to speak to their teachers at the beginning of each school year, perhaps at an orientation or teachers' in-service day.

Most teachers will probably be understanding about your illness and realize that you may sometimes feel tired or need to be excused from class to rest. They may help you find ways to keep up in class and with homework assignments, in case you're absent due to illness, doctor visits, or hospitalization. Some teachers may not be understanding, and if this happens, be sure to speak up. Let the teacher know that you're doing your best and, though you don't expect special treatment, you may need to find creative ways to work around your illness. If the teacher still doesn't seem willing to make accommodations, get your parents involved, talk to your principal, or seek advice from your school counselor.

Another benefit of explaining your illness and treatments to your teachers is that it will save you unwanted embarrassment. You probably don't want to raise your hand each time you need to go to the bathroom or request a hall pass every time you have to see the school nurse to get your medication. If your teachers know that you have a few special needs, you can slip out of class without drawing attention to yourself. This can make life at school a lot less stressful.

If you're thinking that it's probably easier to just keep your teachers in the dark about your illness, remember that they aren't mind readers. If they don't know why you're absent, why you haven't completed all of your homework assignments, or why your grades have been slipping, they may assume that you just don't care about your school work. Your teachers may notice that you're not paying close attention in class or participating as much as you have in the past. It's important for them to understand that you're not "being lazy" or "not applying yourself," but they won't know unless you communicate with them.

What can your teachers do to make your school life more bearable when you're sick or coping with your illness? Perhaps they can help you find ways to complete unfinished assignments, work with a tutor, or make up missed tests. Some teachers may be able to spend time after school working with you one-on-one to catch up. Ask your teachers if it's okay for you to leave class once in a while to go to the school nurse's office to rest and recharge your batteries. Some schools have a homebound program especially for students who have extended absences (for example, if you're in the hospital for a couple of weeks). With the homebound program, a teacher visits you at home to tutor you, give you tests, and keep you up to date on assignments and class work. (Don't knock it—my homebound teacher in seventh grade was the most handsome teacher in the school, and the other girls in my class were trying to figure out how *they* could get involved in the homebound program!)

Physical Education Teachers

Many people who have a chronic illness view their physical education teachers as the enemy—after all, these are the teachers who demand the most from you physically. How will your gym teacher know about any physical limitations you may have if you don't speak up? To have a good relationship with your gym teacher, you need to be honest about what you can and can't do. Let your teacher know that you'll always do as much as you can, but you may need to sit out during some activities or miss class altogether on days when you're really feeling bad. Most physical education teachers are very understanding about this type of thing, so don't worry that your teacher will think you're just trying to get out of class. Work with your teacher so that you can still meet the requirements of the class without putting too much strain on your body.

Your gym teacher should receive a copy of your Care Sheet (see page 162 for an example). Imagine how scary it would be for your teacher and the rest of the class if you suddenly got sick out on the field or court. The sheet will keep your gym teacher informed not only about what to do in an emergency, but also about any physical restrictions you may have.

Your School Counselor

School counselors are there to help you cope with the emotional aspects of school life, so don't hesitate to talk to a counselor about what you're dealing with. A common misconception is that people only go to counselors if "something is wrong with them." In reality, counselors are available for many needs—advice, encouragement, support, and problem-solving. Counselors are trained to listen, and they keep your discussions confidential, so don't be afraid to open up. Let your school counselor know about your illness and how it affects you at school and at home. You may even start to view your school counselor as a friend you can trust with all sorts of personal information.

If you're struggling with some really tough problems, your school counselor is a helpful resource and can offer guidance when you need it most. It takes a strong person to handle things alone, but an even stronger person to ask for help. School counselors can refer you to other helping resources, such as a family therapist, social worker, or psychologist.

Extracurricular Activities

Many young people with chronic illnesses can manage school, clubs, homework, and a part-time job. How do they do it all? Planning. The key is having a manageable schedule and not over-committing yourself. Don't be afraid to say no when it comes to taking on one more activity. If your schedule gets too hectic, slow down and figure out which activities you enjoy most. Eliminate those that aren't as fun or meaningful, and don't feel guilty about it. If you spread yourself too thin, trying to do a little of everything (a job, a volunteer activity, several clubs), you might get frustrated or fatigued. The most important items on your schedule are 1) taking care of yourself, and 2) following your treatment.

Whether you're involved in sports, a job, theater, or other activities, talk to the adults in charge—your coach, boss, director, advisor, etc.—about your illness and how it affects your energy level and everyday life. They'll appreciate knowing about your situation and will have a better understanding of your needs. You may want to provide a copy of your Care Sheet, too, in case of an emergency.

Let your doctor know about your activities to make sure that they aren't too physically demanding. If your treatment or medication schedule interferes with your after-school activities, it may be possible for your doctor to make some special arrangements so you can remain healthy *and* active.

Battling a Fear of Hospitals

"Nothing in life is to be feared. It is only to be understood."
Marie Curie

Without a doubt, the hospital can be a scary place, and it's natural to feel anxious about being hospitalized. Not only are the surroundings unfamiliar, but you may also be facing medical tests and procedures that are painful and frightening. While you're at the hospital, you'll probably see people who are very sick, which can cause you to feel worried and alone. One way to deal with hospitalization is to remember that hospitals are very supportive places where you'll be taken care of by trained people who want to help you get better. Another good way to cope with your fears is to face them. Following are seven of the most common fears about hospitalization and how you can cope.

Fear #1: Pain

One of the scariest things about being in the hospital is pain. *What will it feel like to have an IV? What kinds of tests and procedures will the*

167

doctor have to perform? Will the surgery hurt? Whenever possible, your doctor will tell you beforehand about tests, procedures, and surgery. You may feel that the less you know about these things, the less you'll have to fear. Actually, the opposite is true. It's scarier *not* knowing what's going to happen to you because you'll most likely imagine the worst. Once you know and understand the procedures and how they can help you, you may be less afraid. Unfortunately, being aware of what's going to happen won't *prevent* pain, but the doctors and nurses will try their best to make you comfortable. Your short-term pain is meant to help bring long-term relief from pain and other symptoms.

You may be scared (even terrified) of shots and IVs. Maybe you have a general fear of needles. Needles aren't any fun, but some needles (like those used for blood tests) are so small that the pain is minimal and doesn't last long. If you're going to be stuck with a bigger needle, a nurse may first give you a tiny shot or smear of numbing cream to help deaden the pain when the needle is inserted. When it comes to having an IV, understanding how one works can help ease your fears. An IV is inserted into a vein in your body (usually in your arm) with a needle that's taped in place for as long as you need the IV. The needle is connected to a tube and an IV bag full of medication, liquid nutrition, or blood—whatever your body needs. A computer attached to the IV regulates the amount of liquid that's pumped from the bag into your body. When the needle is first inserted, you may feel some pain for a few seconds, but it soon disappears; if it doesn't, ask a nurse to move the IV to another spot so you'll be more comfortable.

Many people hold their breath during painful procedures, but this isn't a good idea because when you feel fear, you tend to clench and tighten the muscles, making the pain even worse. To manage your pain, instead of holding your breath and tightening up, try to relax and breathe deeply—in through your nose for five seconds and out your mouth for five more seconds. Another way to deal with pain is to squeeze someone's hand, which helps release tension.

Reach out to a family member or friend, or even the nurse or technician, as the test or procedure is performed, and continue your deep breathing so you don't end up holding your breath. If you don't want to hold someone's hand, you can substitute a pillow, blanket, or favorite stuffed animal—anything that's soft and easy to grip. (I've decided that you're never too old to need a stuffed animal. Every time I go to the hospital, my friend Dietrich—a stuffed dog that my parents gave me for my tenth birthday—comes with me. Whenever I'm in pain, I hold on to Dietrich, and sometimes I even take him with me for X-rays and other tests.) One last way to deal with pain is to distract yourself. Hum a tune, picture yourself in an island paradise, or think of anything to get your mind off your discomfort. The more you focus on the pain, the more it will hurt. Remember that the pain is only temporary and tell yourself, "In just a little bit, this will all be over."

For many complicated procedures, including surgery, you'll be given anesthesia to make you sleep. Often, the anesthesia will be injected right into your IV tube, and you won't even feel it going in. If you're having a procedure or test, you may be given light anesthesia, which should numb you and make you feel very happy. For surgery, you'll most likely be given enough anesthesia to make you unconscious. During surgery, the anesthesiologist will monitor you to make sure that you're receiving just enough to keep you from waking up during the surgery or prevent you from falling into too deep of a sleep. After surgery, you'll wake up in a recovery room, and you may be sleepy, confused, and sick to your stomach. Surgery and other procedures can tire you out for a number of days, weeks, or sometimes even months, while your body adjusts to the changes that have occurred.

If you're nervous about surgery (and who isn't?), keep in mind that when you wake up, it will all be over. While you're asleep, an experienced team of surgeons, nurses, and an anesthesiologist will be taking care of you. Once you wake up, the worst is over, and you can focus on getting better.

Fear #2: Being Surrounded by Strangers

You'll meet many new people in the hospital, including doctors, nurses, and technicians (people who take X-rays, draw blood samples, and perform other tests). These strangers will be in and out of your hospital room day and night, and all this activity can be unsettling. The good news is, these people are trained to take care of you—they understand that you're sick, and their job is to help you get better.

Your regular doctor will probably come to visit you in the hospital to monitor your progress and talk about how you're feeling. If your doctor can't get to the hospital every day, another doctor will check on you and report to your doctor. If you're going to have surgery, your surgeon will visit you, too. Occasionally, a doctor may want to bring in one or two medical students because an important part of their education is to examine real patients. Take advantage of these doctor visits to ask questions about your treatment and hospital stay.

Nurses are the people you'll see most often. Hospitals usually have three groups of nurses—those who work in the morning, in the afternoon, and through the night. You'll probably be treated by the same nurses every day (except for weekends). Nurses provide constant care, and they'll be in and out of your room all the time, checking on you, taking your temperature and blood pressure, and giving you your medication. In my experience, most nurses will do as much as possible to make your hospital stay comfortable, and they'll take the time to talk with you and help you in any way they can.

At some point during your stay, you may also meet a dietitian, who will make sure that you're getting the nutrition you need. If you're able to eat solid foods, you may be able to select your meals from a pre-planned menu—it's not homecooking, but it's supposed to be good for you.

Unless you're in intensive care, a section of the hospital reserved for people who are very sick and need a lot of attention, you'll probably have a roommate. Your roommate may have the same illness or one completely different from yours. More often than not, roommates are the same gender, so you probably won't share a room with someone of the opposite sex. If you're in the pediatric section, your roommate will be another young person; if you're in another section of the hospital, your roommate may be an adult. There's a curtain between the beds that you can close when you want privacy and open when you and your roommate want to visit. You and your roommate can be a source of strength for each other, but if you really don't want a roommate, you may be able to get a single room (they're usually more expensive, so talk to your parents about whether your insurance company covers the additional costs).

While you're at the hospital, you're going to run into other patients besides your roommate. It can be scary, not to mention depressing, to be around so many strangers who are sick. They probably don't want to be in the hospital any more than you do, and they may feel just as uncomfortable about being surrounded by others who are ill. While this may sound strange, I've found that the hospital can be a good place to meet people. I don't mean that you should hang out there on Friday nights, but if you're in the hospital for more than a few days, talking to other patients your age can make you feel less lonely and bored.

Fear #3: Being Away from Friends, Family, and Pets

It's hard to be away from the people you love. Luckily, hospitals have visiting hours so your friends and family can come to see you, and once the doctor says it's okay for you to have visitors, anyone can drop by. Your visitors can bring a deck of cards, puzzles, a photo of your pet, or anything else to get your mind off your hospital stay. It's not a good idea, though, to have a whole bunch of people in your hospital room all at once because you'll probably get worn out.

In some hospitals, parents can visit whenever they want, and family members usually are allowed longer visiting hours. If your room is big enough, the nurses may be able to provide a fold-up bed so you can have a parent stay overnight. You'll feel a lot better just knowing someone you love is close by.

When you're in the hospital, you may want to have a parent spend *every* night with you, but, depending on your family situation, this may not always be possible. If you don't like being alone at night, do something to keep your mind occupied (read, watch TV, play a hand-held video game, write letters, do homework, or work on puzzles).

You may discover that some of your friends aren't comfortable visiting you in the hospital. While this may hurt your feelings, try to understand. Perhaps their only experiences in the hospital have been negative, or maybe they associate hospitals with death. If your friends are too young to drive, they may not be able to visit you for transportation reasons. You'll most likely have a phone in your room, so you can make and receive calls whenever you want. Long distance calls are added to your hospital bill, so check with your parents first.

Remind yourself that your stay is temporary. You won't be in the hospital forever, and soon you'll be back at home with the people you love. Take this time to relax, regain your strength, and get better.

Fear #4: Loss of Control

One of the things I hated most about being in the hospital was not being able to take care of myself. For a while, I couldn't even sit up or roll over without someone helping me. It's very frustrating to have to rely on others for everything, but you can't help it. Instead of worrying about not being in control, focus on your recovery (and enjoy being waited on hand and foot!).

Don't feel embarrassed about asking the nurses for help—they understand that you can't do everything on your own while you're recovering. I know how humiliating it can be to call a nurse because you have to go to the bathroom and need help, but nurses deal with that kind of thing every day. No one is going to laugh at you because you can't walk to the bathroom by yourself or need to use a bedpan. At the hospital, more than anyplace else, people understand your limitations.

You may feel more comfortable having a family member, rather than a nurse, help you wash yourself. If a parent isn't present at the time a nurse comes in, you can say you'd like to wait because someone else is going to help you. Don't worry that you're offending the nurses because they understand the discomfort of having a stranger help you do personal things.

If you have an emergency while you're at the hospital, the nurse is just a call button away. The call button will be an easy reach from your bed, and all you have to do is push it when you need something.

Fear #5: Being Bored and "Missing Out"

There you are in your hospital bed, looking at the sunshine outside, feeling bored, and wondering what all your friends are doing at school. It's hard to be stuck indoors, especially when you don't have all of your personal belongings to help keep you occupied. You may worry that you're missing out on all the fun (after-school activities, parties, athletic events) and that everyone will forget you. They won't, though. To pass the time, make the hospital your "home away from home." Ask your family to bring your favorite books, your mail, CDs, board games, pictures of your pets, or anything else that reminds you of home and of your friends. If you don't already use a journal, you might want to start because you'll have lots of free time to write.

If you have a chance to pack before you go to the hospital, I recommend that you bring your pillow and favorite blanket, cozy pajamas, socks, a bathrobe, and some slippers or other footwear that's comfortable. If you have to make an emergency trip to the hospital and don't have time to pack, ask a family member to bring the things you need later. You'll most likely have a small table by your bed, and you can use it to display pictures, cards, flowers, and gifts that you receive while you're in the hospital. Having familiar things in plain view will help make your surroundings more comfortable.

As you begin to recover, you'll be able to move around in the hospital, so you can check out the activity rooms or lounges. Activity rooms often have toys, games, movies, reading materials, and sometimes arts and crafts projects. Being in the hospital can be an opportunity to make new friends—you can meet a lot of cool people just like you who also happen to be patients. Some hospitals have child-life specialists and recreational therapists who are trained to help young people relax in the hospital, so use them as a resource when you're lonely or bored.

Fear #6: Falling Behind in School

At first, you may think, "Hurrah, no school!" Then reality sinks in, and you realize how much school work you'll have to make up after your hospital stay. If you have the energy, you can try to complete some assignments in the hospital, but don't put too much pressure on yourself (no one expects you to come back from a hospital stay with all of your school work completed). Your primary goal should be to recover and to take the best possible care of yourself.

Some hospitals offer tutors for young people who have to stay in the hospital for an extended time. These tutors can help you keep up with your classes while you continue to receive care for your illness. If you need to spend time recovering at home after you leave the hospital, find out if your school has a homebound program so a teacher can work with you one-on-one to help you catch up. If this type of program doesn't exist at your school, you may want to see if your teachers can offer suggestions for getting back on track with your homework, tests, and other assignments.

Fear #7: Going Home

Wait, isn't going home the best part of your hospital stay? Not necessarily. It's common to have mixed feelings about leaving the hospital, especially after you've gotten used to the routines and the constant care. You may worry that you won't be able to handle your recovery on your own, and you may miss the nurses, doctors, and other caregivers who helped you. These feelings probably won't last long. Once you get home, you'll be happy to be in your familiar surroundings with your family close by.

The thought of seeing your friends again can make you anxious. You may wonder if they'll think you look different or if they won't know what to say to you. Although it can be a little awkward at first, seeing your friends is a great way to lift your spirits and make you feel at home again. When you're up to it, plan an informal welcome-back party for yourself and invite a few of your closest friends—they'll be glad that you're back.

Support Groups
and National
Organizations

"By speaking of our misfortunes we often relieve them."
French proverb

Sometimes my family and friends will tell me, "You're going to be okay," and I think to myself, "Yeah, I'm going to be okay, but how would *you* know? You can't possibly understand how I'm feeling." Then I feel guilty for thinking such unfriendly thoughts. The truth is, most people you encounter—friends, family, teachers, classmates, doctors—won't know *exactly* how you feel, even though they're trying their best to understand and to help you. They mean well, but sometimes you just need to talk to someone who really identifies with your symptoms, pain, treatment, and emotions . . . in other words, a person who shares the same illness.

Having a chronic illness can be a major pain in more ways than one, and it's important to have a chance to meet other young people who are dealing with similar issues. Of course, even if you meet someone who has the same illness, you won't necessarily have every symptom and feeling in common. But, in general, other young people with the same chronic illness as you will be a great resource for discussing (and complaining about) the physical and emotional complications that come with a medical problem. Where do you meet these people? Support groups are a great place to start.

Support Groups

In the years after my diagnosis, my mom wanted me to attend a support group meeting. She knew that I needed to talk with other people going through the same things I was. All I could picture was a room full of kids whining about their illnesses. I figured that it was hard enough for me to deal with my own problems, let alone those of other people. Even as I began to face my illness and learn to live with it, I remained reluctant to go to a support group. To me, the words "support group" implied that I couldn't handle my disease by myself. I pictured counselors with soft, low voices saying, "Be a friend to your disease, and your disease will be a friend to you."

Then I went off to college, and I was suddenly hours away from home and from the people who had always been my source of support. One day during freshman orientation, we had a break and a few of us decided to go to the pool to relax. I put on my one-piece bathing suit because I'd vowed never again to wear a bikini (I was afraid that people would take one look at my surgical scars and confuse me with Frankenstein's monster). My roommate and I spread out our towels next to a girl we'd met the day before, and just as I was about to plop down on the ground, I noticed something strange . . . scars. The girl was wearing a two-piece bathing suit, and I saw some familiar scars on her stomach; my hand flew up, and I pointed to them. "What are those?" I asked, rather abruptly. I thought that she had Crohn's disease like me, and since I'd never before met anyone else who had the same illness, I couldn't contain my shock.

"Well," she said, "I had surgery to remove some kind of infection a few years ago." Alarms went off in my head. "What was it?" I said. "I mean, why did you have to have surgery?" She looked at me calmly and explained: "I have an illness that makes me get infections sometimes. I'm taking a really strong medication for it, and the doctors think I'll have to take it forever." I was about to explode. "What is it? What is it called? Don't tell me. . . ." She suddenly seemed to realize what I was getting at, and we simultaneously blurted out, "Crohn's disease!" She leapt up saying, "Oh, my gosh. Are you serious?" I told her I had almost identical scars.

We immediately started talking about how we were diagnosed, what medications we'd tried, and which foods we couldn't eat. We became so absorbed in our conversation that we completely ignored my roommate, who sat there staring at us. "Hello? Excuse me? Guys? What are you talking about?" she asked. We turned to her and said, "We have the same disease! Isn't that cool?" The look on her face made it clear that she didn't quite understand how "disease" could be equated with "cool," but she nodded and smiled. I was so happy that I'd finally met someone I could *really* talk to—someone my age who'd been through almost exactly the same things I'd been through.

This experience made me rethink my attitude toward support groups. If one person could make me feel so much more comfortable with my illness in such a short time, what could a whole group accomplish? I was thankful that I now had a friend who had the same illness as me and understood everything I was dealing with. She was a great resource because my busy college life prevented me from joining a support group. Since then, I've continued to rely on my very understanding family and friends whenever I'm having a hard time. I can't help but think, though, that my teen years would have been easier if I'd taken my mom's advice and joined a support group back then.

◀ Why Support Groups Help ▶

Support groups offer a unique brand of encouragement and, well, support. Group members know what it's like to go through what you're going through, and they also know how hard it can be to open up to others. People in support groups often have good advice for coping with problems—they'll let you know what has and hasn't worked for them.

Give support groups a try. The groups usually involve members who are roughly the same age (children, teens, or adults). You'll be surrounded by your peers—people who speak the same language and who understand the issues you face every day. You may not enjoy your first meeting if you're a little nervous, but stick with it. No one will force you to talk if you don't want to. Once you get to know people, though, you may suddenly feel as if you have a whole room full of friends who understand you and can offer the encouragement you need.

At your support group meetings, feel free to talk about anything—from dealing with your doctor, family, and friends to handling your illness at school. Or, if you want, discuss topics that are completely unrelated to your illness. Sometimes group members talk about their day, an upcoming date, or even movies they've seen. There are no hard-and-fast rules.

Most support groups have one or more coordinators, who may be counselors, physicians, informed parents, or just people who are dealing with the same illness or problem. Coordinators are trained to give information about the illness, answer questions, provide encouragement for group members, and plan and run the meetings. Some support group coordinators even offer support outside of regular meetings and are available to talk over the phone.

How do you find a support group once you decide to join one? Call Information? Look in the Yellow Pages? Hire a private investigator? Actually, it's simple: Get in touch with the national organization(s) dedicated to providing information and support for your particular illness. National organizations (read more about them on pages 181–184) are usually made up of many smaller chapters all over the country, and once you contact an organization, you'll receive information about your local chapter. Your local chapter can refer you to the nearest support groups and tell you where and when they meet, who coordinates them, and how to contact the coordinators. Some groups are sponsored by the national organization, and others are started by patients themselves.

It's possible that, after a few support group meetings, you still may not feel comfortable among the members. This doesn't mean you should abandon support groups forever. See if you can find a different one, and give the new group a fair shot. You may have to travel a little farther to attend a different group, but if you find one that makes you feel more comfortable, it will be worth it.

Check It Out

The American Self-Help Clearinghouse offers information on a huge number of self-help groups throughout the U.S. Staffers can provide contact information for national groups or tell you about regional clearinghouses. If you can't find a local group for your illness, the Clearinghouse may be able to put you in touch with other people who want to start a group. If you're online, you can find a version of the *Self-Help Sourcebook* that includes information on getting in touch with other people who want to start a support group, finding a meeting place, and running meetings.

American Self-Help Clearinghouse
St. Clare's Health Services
25 Pocono Road
Denville, NJ 07834
(973) 625-7101
FAX: (973) 625-8848
http://www.cmhc.com/selfhelp/

National Organizations

National organizations not only connect you to support groups and physicians but may also provide informational materials about your illness (usually free of charge). Because these organizations usually stay informed about the latest treatments and research for specific illnesses, you can use them as a resource when you want to learn more about your health. If you contact an organization but can't get the information you're looking for, the staffers may be able to suggest other sources.

To find out about national organizations related to your illness, ask your doctor for recommendations or call local hospitals for help. You'll find the names and addresses of national organizations for specific illnesses after each story in Part 1 of this book; on pages 182–184 is a list of general health-care organizations. If you have access to the Internet and a browser, just type in the name of your illness and see what comes up—if there's a national organization for your illness, you'll probably find it. You can also go to the library for information.

Once you've found a national organization that you'd like to get in touch with, you can call, write, or fax them; some organizations even have Web sites with email access. Ask if the organization has a free "information packet" (pamphlets and brochures about your illness and the organization). If the organization you're contacting doesn't have information packets, request a list of printed materials so you can choose those you'd like to order. Some organizations charge a small fee for materials, but many are free. Your initial request for information will probably put you on the organization's mailing list, in which case you'll receive new materials—often flyers and newsletters—every few weeks or months. If the organization sponsors a support group, ask for the name and phone number of the coordinator in your area.

Organizations

American Academy of Child and Adolescent Psychiatry
3615 Wisconsin Avenue, NW
Washington, D.C. 20016-3007
1-800-333-7636
(202) 966-7300
FAX: (202) 966-2891
http://www.aacap.org

This professional medical organization advocates for mental health issues, establishes professional standards, and promotes mental health research. It also educates the general public on mental health and offers a number of publications, brochures, audiotapes, and other materials (some free of charge) for this purpose. AACAP staffers can provide referrals to doctors throughout the United States.

American Chronic Pain Association
P.O. Box 850
Rocklin, CA 95677
(916) 632-0922
FAX: (916) 632-3208

This self-help group encourages those who live with pain to take an active role in its management. The ACPA offers positive and con-structive methods of dealing with pain, sponsors support groups, and publishes a newsletter and other materials. The ACPA also has over 800 chapters around the world and organizes a pen-pal program for young people.

Association for the Care of Children's Health
19 Mantua Road
Mount Royal, NJ 08061
(609) 224-1742
FAX: (609) 423-3420
http://www.acch.org

The ACCH links people from a variety of medical and professional disciplines, parents, public policy makers, and community activists in an effort to improve children's health. The organization offers brochures, books, videos, and audiotapes on a wide range of health issues, including chronic illnesses. Check out the ACCH Web site for a list of publications, health information, and links to lots of other health-related organizations.

Fanlight Productions
4196 Washington Street, Suite 2
Boston, MA 02131
1-800-937-4113 (U.S. only)
(617) 469-4999
FAX: (617) 469-3379
http://www.fanlight.com

This company produces films and videos on health-care issues and chronic illnesses, including epilepsy, diabetes, and cancer. You can find several titles for young people.

Friends' Health Connection
P.O. Box 114
New Brunswick, NJ 08903
1-800-48-FRIEND
http://www.48friend.com

This organization was founded by twenty-five-year-old Roxanne Black, who has lupus. The Friends' Health Connection puts people who have (or have overcome) a disease, illness, or disability in touch with others who have experienced the same condition so they can offer mutual support.

National Heart, Lung, and Blood Institute Information Center
P.O. Box 30105
Bethesda, MD 20824-0105
1-800-575-WELL (Heart disease information line)
(301) 592-8573
FAX: (301) 592-8563
http://www.nhlbi.nih.gov

Sponsored by the National Institutes of Health, this organization plans and conducts research of heart, lung, and blood disorders. You can receive informational materials (many are free of charge) about heart, lung, and blood disorders and their treatments. Check out the Center's huge Web site, which contains health news, online fact sheets, and links to many other government-sponsored health resources.

National Self-Help Clearinghouse
Graduate School and University Center of the City University of
New York
25 West 43rd Street, Suite 620
New York, NY 10036
(212) 354-8525
FAX: (212) 642-1956
http://www.selfhelpweb.org

This organization offers information on self-help groups throughout
the U.S., conducts research on the effects of self-help, sponsors
training for self-help group leaders, and provides information about
and referral to self-help groups and regional clearinghouses.

Web Site

Bandaides and Blackboards
http://funrsc.fairfield.edu/~jfleitas/contents.html

This site includes helpful tips for taking medication and talking to your
friends about your illness, games, poems, fun graphics, art, photos,
essays, and true stories from other young people with chronic illnesses.

Books

The Essential Guide to Chronic Illness by James W. Long, M.D. (NY:
HarperCollins, 1997). This reader-friendly handbook by a doctor of
internal medicine profiles 47 chronic illnesses. It includes information
on symptoms, treatments, the number of people who have each illness,
and more. You'll also find resources for medical and support organizations for each illness.

The Self-Help Sourcebook: Finding and Forming Mutual Aid Self-Help Groups,
edited by Barbara J. White and Edward J. Madara (Denville, NJ: The
American Self-Help Clearinghouse, 1997). The sixth edition of this
resource includes over 700 groups and hundreds of phone numbers you
can call for further information on specific self-help topics. You'll learn
how to start a group of your own and participate in online groups.

Your Future

"I have discovered in life that there are ways of getting almost anywhere you want to go, if you really want to go."
Langston Hughes

You're at an age when your life is changing, sometimes dramatically, every day. Before long, you'll begin to make plans for your future. Once you leave high school, you may attend college, get a full-time job, or go to a vocational school. Whatever you choose to do, you'll be gaining new responsibilities, but your main one will continue to be managing your health. Although your parents, relatives, friends, and other people who care about you may still be available for support and advice, you'll be making many decisions on your own, and *you* will be the one in charge of your future. The skills that help you manage your illness today will continue to help you, regardless of your long-term plans.

Think of your coping skills as a savings account. With a savings account, you usually start out with very little money, but you gradually make deposits—some of them so small that you may think they're meaningless. Over time, as you check your balance, you start to realize that each deposit has made a difference and your account has grown significantly. Dealing with a chronic illness is similar. You build coping skills over the years, adding new ones (big or small) a little at time. Your skills build you into a stronger person and help you to survive and thrive. Eventually, you can look back and realize just how far you've really come.

When you're an adult, managing your illness is *really* up to you. If you start taking some responsibility for this as a child or a teenager, it will be that much easier when you're on your own—living in an apartment or a house, going to work every day, and generally running your life. Each day brings new challenges, but your future is bright. You can manage your illness and live a happy, healthy life. It happened for me, and I know it can happen for you, too. Following are some of the challenges you may face in your future and some advice for meeting each one successfully.

Finding a New Doctor

If you intend to move away from home, you'll probably need to find a new doctor. I went to college two hours away from my parents' house and, for a year, tried to keep the same doctor because I thought it would be too much of a hassle to start over again with a new one. I learned how difficult it could be to coordinate doctor visits with trips home. After asking my doctor to recommend a specialist near my school, I got a new doctor right across the street from my college dormitory. I could walk to the office and was able to schedule appointments at times that were convenient for me.

Another reason for finding a doctor close to you is the chance of an emergency. I went to the emergency room twice while I was away at college, and both times, my new doctor was paged and came to the hospital to see me. You'll feel a lot better knowing that your doctor is able to take care of you personally. Since college, I've moved several times to different locations and apartments. Each time I move, I make it a priority to find a new local doctor and a nearby pharmacy so I can pick up my prescriptions easily. I always make sure to keep my cellular phone with me, too—not only for business but in case I have a medical emergency or simply need to call my doctor.

If you're planning to move, ask your current doctor to recommend a physician in your new area or try calling a national organization* that deals with your illness to see if staffers can offer a referral for a local doctor. Be sure to mention if you prefer a male or female doctor.

Going to College or Vocational School

Many of the coping skills that help you in middle school and high school will assist you in college or vocational school, too. Let people know about your illness—talk to the campus nurse, your coach if you're involved in sports, your professors, the dean, your roommate, or any other people you think should know. Give each person a copy of your Care Sheet** so you can get the help you need in case of an emergency.

Your relationships with your professors will probably be much different from those you've had with your high school teachers. Although your professors will care about you and want you to succeed, they'll treat you like an adult, not a child. They'll expect you to take responsibility for showing up for class and completing papers, tests, exams, and assignments on time. There probably won't be a roll call or attendance check, and you won't receive a detention or other punishment for skipping class. If your illness is causing repeated absences or affecting your performance in class, it's up to you to let your professors know. Together, you and your professor can come up with ways to meet your class requirements. Don't think of it as asking for "special help." You have the right to

*For more on national organizations, see "Support Groups and National Organizations," pp. 176–184.
**For more on Care Sheets, see pp. 161–162.

be on equal ground with other students, but your illness may sometimes put you at a disadvantage; asking for what you need (a revised deadline, a make-up exam) simply puts you back on equal ground. If a friend had the flu, wouldn't you advise her to ask for extra time on her assignments, rather than take a lower grade because she had the misfortune of becoming ill?

It's also important to communicate with your roommate, friends, classmates, and other peers about your illness. When you go away to school, your new friends can become a second family (your "family away from home"). Your illness isn't a dark secret, and to build a support system for yourself, you'll need to tell your friends about your health problem. Be prepared to answer a lot of questions if your friends are curious. Because people are a little bit older and wiser after high school, they should be mature enough to handle your news without judging you or dropping you as a friend. Give your new friends a chance to be there for you when you need them most—more often than not, they'll come through.

Getting a Job

If you're entering the workforce, you'll be meeting many new people, and it's up to you to decide who you'd like to tell about your illness. In case you have an emergency at work, people need to know what to do, so it wouldn't hurt to keep a copy of your Care Sheet in your personnel file.*

You may fear that telling your boss about your illness will prevent you from being hired or give the impression that you can't handle the job. Because laws protect people with chronic illnesses or other "disabilities" from discrimination in the workplace, a prospective employer can't refuse to hire you because of your illness. It's your decision when to tell prospective employers, but it

*For more on Care Sheets, see pp. 161–162.

may be awkward to mention your illness right after you're hired ("By the way, I have a chronic illness that sometimes makes me have to go to the hospital and miss work, but no big deal, right? Can I have next Monday off?"). If you're really interested in a certain company, have made it past the first round of interviews, and are invited back for a second interview, you may want to mention your illness then. Just explain that you have a chronic illness but are able to manage it effectively. You don't have to go into great detail or be embarrassed to speak up. If you're the right person for the position, you'll probably get the job.

Forming New Relationships

You may ask yourself, "Who would ever want to date me or have a serious relationship with me? No one wants to be involved with someone who has an illness." This couldn't be further from the truth. I've had boyfriends, and I'm currently in a serious relationship with someone I care a lot about—and who really cares about me.

That doesn't mean that your relationships will always be easy. Like everyone else, I've had good relationships and bad, and each one has been a learning experience. Give yourself room to make a few bad choices or mistakes. My very first boyfriend, for example, didn't ever want to talk about my illness, which really made me feel uncomfortable (like I had to hide it). I realized that he didn't want to know the real me. I became more selective about who I dated, and one thing that helped me was to only get involved with guys who would like me for *me*—illness and all.

I'm honest with them, and I explain my illness and how it affects me. I've found this is the best way to ensure that there are no surprises later in the relationship. You may wonder if telling a guy or girl you like about your illness will only scare the person away. You can't be 100 percent sure how people will react, but sooner or later the truth has to come out. Once you find someone you're interested in, let the relationship develop a bit and then be open about your illness. You deserve to be with someone who not only accepts you but appreciates you, too.

The most wonderful thing is to find someone who really cares about you and understands what you're going through. When I had surgery for my Crohn's, my boyfriend at the time came to the hospital to visit me every chance he got. He sat by my bed and held my hand as I slept. He saw the worst of my illness—I had tubes coming out of my nose, was as white as the sheets I was laying in, and couldn't sit up because my stomach muscles had been cut during surgery. I thought my boyfriend would never be attracted to me again, but he actually told me he was *more* attracted to me after the surgery because I'd let him share such a personal part of my life. What I've learned is that when the emotional relationship is solid, the physical attraction is all the more meaningful.

Someday you might even consider marriage. Don't let your chronic illness stop you. If you're also thinking about having children, it's a good idea to talk to your doctor first so you can find out about any limitations you might have as a result of your illness. Don't worry about it too much, though. More often than not, it's very possible to have successful physical relationships and to eventually have children. Face these challenges as you do all others regarding your health—one day at a time.

▲▼▲▼▲▼▲▼

Don't fear the future or worry about things that may never happen. I know that I might have a flare-up at any time or need more surgery. Yet, I still go to my job and work hard, spend time with my friends and family, travel, pursue my interests, enjoy meeting new people, and look forward to each day. Though you may be on your own, you're not alone—there are people who care about you, and you can ask them for help when you need it. Trust yourself enough to know that, whatever happens, you'll be able to handle it. Make the most of your life.

Final Thoughts

"You cannot create experience. You must undergo it."
Albert Camus

I hope this book has helped you realize there are others like you. Yes, you may be different—but so is everyone in some way or another. Your illness is part of you, so don't fight it. Instead, fight the urge to give up. Challenge anyone who says that you can't fulfill your dreams. Having an illness may mean that you have to find new ways to achieve your goals, but you can do it. This is who you are.

Jonathan Miller, a psychologist and author, once said, "An illness is not something a person has. It is another way of being."

How will *you* be?

Index

About the Author

Kelly Huegel received her undergraduate degree in English and secondary education in 1996 from Hood College in Frederick, Maryland, and was a recent recipient of the college's Outstanding Recent Graduate Award. She was selected for the University of Denver's Publishing Institute, where she began to develop the idea for *Young People and Chronic Illness.* Her hope is that this book will provide the encouragement and advice that she wishes she'd had during the first years after her diagnosis of Crohn's disease. Currently, Kelly works as an editor at the National Academy Press, a scholarly publisher in Washington, D.C. Now 25, Kelly has been successfully managing her chronic illness with drug therapy for the last eight years. She enjoys playing tennis, reading, cooking, traveling, shopping, and spending time with her friends and family. Along with her career in publishing, Kelly plans to continue writing for a young audience.

Other Great Books from Free Spirit

Making Every Day Count
Daily Readings for Young People on Solving Problems,
Setting Goals, & Feeling Good About Yourself
by Pamela Espeland and Elizabeth Verdick
Each entry in this book of daily readings includes a
thought-provoking quotation, a brief essay, and a
positive "I"-statement that relates the entry to the
reader's own life. For ages 11 & up.
$9.95; 392 pp.; softcover; 4¼" x 6¼"

When Nothing Matters Anymore
A Survival Guide for Depressed Teens
by Bev Cobain, R.N.,C.
Written for teens with depression—and those who feel
despondent, dejected, or alone—this powerful book
offers help, hope, and potentially life-saving facts and
advice. Includes survival tips, resources, true stories
from teens who have dealt with depression, and more.
For ages 13 & up.
$13.95; 176 pp.; softcover; illus.; 6" x 9"

Fighting Invisible Tigers
A Stress Management Guide for Teens
Revised & Updated
by Earl Hipp
Proven, practical advice for teens on coping with stress,
being assertive, building relationships, taking risks,
making decisions, dealing with fears, and more.
For ages 11 & up.
$10.95; 160 pp.; softcover; illus.; 6" x 9"

*To place an order or to request a free catalog of
SELF–HELP FOR KIDS® and SELF–HELP FOR TEENS® materials,
please write, call, email, or visit our Web site:*

Free Spirit Publishing Inc.
400 First Avenue North • Suite 616 • Minneapolis, MN 55401-1724
toll-free 800.735.7323 • local 612.338.2068 • fax 612.337.5050
help4kids@freespirit.com • www.freespirit.com